Acknowledgments

They say it takes a village to raise a child. I also believe it takes a village to raise a book from concept to print.

To that village I owe a great debt.

At the risk of forgetting some names, I want to specifically thank some of those who made this journey possible.

Thank you to Josh Dorkin for creating BiggerPockets, which I attribute the bulk of my success thus far to. Additionally, thank you for the guidance in creating and publishing this book and, of course, for the excellent foreword.

Thank you J Scott for your amazing *Book on Flipping Houses* that opened the door for this publication. Thank you Mike Simmons, Chad Carson, Douglas Larson, Ben Leybovich, Michael Blank, Sharon Vornholt, Tim Gordon, Jerry Puckett, Aaron Mazzrillo, and Jaren Barnes for your wisdom and time given to help make this book launch a success.

Thank you Sharon Tzib and Seamane Flanagan for your work on editing this book. I would not want to be the person responsible for cleaning up my mess, but you two did amazing things. And Maher Abiad- your ability to turn my text into an amazing audiobook will open up this book to so many more people, so thank you.

Thank you to the BiggerPockets community for your wisdom and advice over the past seven yearsl, and thank you to all my family and friends who have offered support and encouragement through this crazy journey.

Finally, thank you to my Papa, for blessing me more than any man should ever be blessed.

Thank you all.

Dedication

Creative real estate investing is never easy, but often filled with uncertainty, stress, and a healthy dose of hard work. Therefore, this book is dedicated to the woman who stuck by me through every difficult moment and offered life saving insights at every step. For Heather, my bride.

Table of Contents

Foreword

Joshua Dorkin
CEO, BiggerPockets

"I am not a teacher, but an awakener." — Robert Frost

If you're thinking that one book can deliver all your hopes and dreams, you may be right; if you find that book, please get in touch and share it with me.

While this book can certainly equip you well for the journey, it is wholly up to you to create your own path to success. It won't necessarily be easy, but I think Theodore Roosevelt nailed it when he said, "Nothing in the world is worth having or worth doing unless it means effort, pain, difficulty."

This book is not designed to give you one simple formula for investing success -- or even to concede that such a formula exists. Rather, this book is designed to teach you a variety of strategies and concepts so you can learn to think outside the box and craft your own personal strategy for no money down investing. It's designed to open your mind to new ways of thinking, not to force any particular master plan down your throat. As such, this book does not offer overnight success or instant riches, but it does promise skills and knowledge that will serve you the rest of your investing career (and life) -- if you so choose.

As any experienced real estate investor can tell you, there are no "secrets," and there are no systems that work all the time. Real estate investing is not black and white; it's not a button that can be pressed or an ATM machine that shoots out cash if the right combination of numbers are pressed. Real estate is a complex, multi-dimensional maze where success requires far more than a script, workbook and seminar, no matter what late night TV gurus might proclaim.

It was my exposure to these such gurus that initially set me on the journey that eventually spurred the beginnings of BiggerPockets. As a brand new real estate investor, I took to the internet to find solutions for the problems with tenants, properties and property managers I'd been handling. Instead of unearthing a wealth of thoughtful discussions, I discovered that the real estate industry was dominated by gurus who offered assistance only via overpriced and heavily hyped programs.

Something needed to change...and out of this necessity, BiggerPockets.com was born. Soon, tens of thousands (now tens of millions!) began to flock to the site, attracted to the community-based education that focused on the people, not the product.

A grassroots movement had been born.

An active member of the BiggerPockets community from the start, Brandon Turner approached me several years ago to write for the site's blog. Though I knew little about him at the time, his writing intrigued me, and I took a chance on him as a contributor to our platform. A few months later, I again took a chance when I hired him to become our lead editor and community manager.

It was a chance that paid off.

Brandon is a natural leader who captivated the imagination of our community. Aside from his behind-the-scenes work to cultivate the site, Brandon continues to lend his unique and insightful voice to our blog and podcast, and he is an active part of our investing community. Just as impressively, he has spent the better part of the decade building a portfolio of real estate encompassing dozens of units without any of his own money. He has shown incredible resourcefulness in his ability to acquire both rental properties and flips using other people's capital, steadily growing his portfolio year by year.

This is why when Brandon approached me to write a book about the real estate investing strategies he has used that rely on creativity rather than cash, I was excited. Still, I had one major hesitation...

The Problem with No Money Down

I've always been bothered by the "no money down" books, CDs and seminars prevalent in the real estate industry. Typically, the evangelists for these strategies claim to know some secret method that will help you find wild success through real estate with no money, no time and no risk. These "no money down secrets" are designed to lure people into the belief that real estate investing is easy and lucrative if only someone follows this one exact step-by-step system.

Despite my irritations with the "no money down" culture, the concept does intrigue me. After all, it is the lack of capital that keeps most from ever entering the world of real estate investing, which is sad. Real estate can have such a powerful impact on a person's future, so the idea that you can enter the game without having a war chest of cash is especially exciting.

But here is the truth that the late-night infomercial hosts don't want you to know: There is no one easy secret system that people are using to invest with no money down. In fact, nearly every creative real estate investor I have met in my almost 10 years of running BiggerPockets has a unique twist in how they finance their deals -- and no one says it's easy.

The Truth About Creative Investing

It is this truth that sets this book above any other creative real estate book ever written. You see, this book is not about some secret system. It's not about complicated strategies that you need to pay $9997 to discover. To be honest, it's not even designed to tell you what to do.

Every market is different, every investor is different, every investment is different. So how can one system offer an answer? It can't, and that's why this book is only the beginning. I encourage you to not only read, but to engage with the content. Internalize it; make it your own. Then take action.

This is not a recipe book, this is an art class…and school is now in session.

Don't let this book be another a collector on your shelf. Let this book be the catalyst you need to take a leap of faith, map out a bright future all your own and see what lies beyond the cubicle walls.

Josh Dorkin

BiggerPockes Founder and CEO

CHAPTER ONE: THE ART OF CREATIVE REAL ESTATE INVESTING

Allow me to start this book talking about one of my favorite things: pizza.

Sure, it may seem like a rather absurd way to start a book on buying real estate with little to no money down, but bear with me a moment, and it will all make sense.

When I go to the pizza store to pick up a pepperoni pizza with extra cheese, I have one choice: to pay for it with my hard-earned money. I suppose I have other choices, but I'd rather avoid the orange jumpsuit and forced community service involved in theft.

However, the rules for real estate investing are actually not as hard and demanding as those for buying pizza or other consumer goods, so you'll have many more options. Better yet, those options are not only legal, they are also a lot of fun to learn and apply. I call this process "creative real estate investing."

One of my favorite aspects of real estate investing is the ability to trade cash for creativity. In my world, this is the truest definition of creative real estate investing.

You can't easily do this with stocks, mutual funds, gold, or most other kinds of investments. If you wanted to buy gold but had only $1,000 to spend, you would probably buy just $1,000 worth. If the price of gold then doubled over the next decade, you would make only another $1,000 in that ten-year time frame. If it doubled again the following decade, you would then have $4,000 in your portfolio.

You can imagine how long building serious wealth might take with this method, especially with the market fluctuating so greatly. In fact, gold has done tremendous things over the past decade, climbing from $282 per ounce in February of 2000 to over $1,300 per ounce in February of 2014. While that rise may seem incredible, it's only incredible for those who had a significant amount of money to invest to begin with. After all, if you had bought that $1,000 worth of gold in 2000, today you'd have approximately $4,600—hardly anything to quit your job over.

The same applies to the stock market. And mutual funds. And fine wine. And nearly all other investments.

Now, there's nothing wrong with investing in those other things (and in fact, I recommend a "balanced diet" with respect to investments), but if you have little or no money, getting started can take a *long* time.

Frustrating, isn't it?

However, with real estate, you can leverage your knowledge, time, and creativity to essentially make money from *nothing*. This is what creative finance is all about: replacing cash with creativity, money with motivation, and dollars with determination.

Do you have that creativity, that motivation, that determination? If so, you can do some amazing things to improve your family's financial future. If not, don't worry. This book will show you the way.

Who Am I?

My name is Brandon, and I'm addicted to creative real estate investing.

I started investing in real estate at the age of 21 with no credit, no cash, and—honestly—no idea what I was doing. However, I had decided that I was going to be a real estate investor come hell or high water, so that's what I set out to do. I read every book the regional library system had on real estate investing, spoke with every real estate investor I could find in my area, attended landlord meetings to network, and continued to work my day job making barely above minimum wage for the first few years.

I jumped into the world of creative finance because, frankly, I was broke.

Fast forward seven years and I'm not a millionaire, I don't drive a fancy car (unless you consider my 2007 Prius fancy, which, with its 49 MPG, I definitely would), and I've made more mistakes in real estate than I'd like to admit. However, I've also amassed a portfolio of rental units and flipped or wholesaled a variety of properties that have provided me with enough income to support my family whether I maintain a day job or not—and I've purchased every property using little or no money of my own.

I don't say this to brag. The truth is, I didn't jump into creative finance because I was some super genius or because I was trying to achieve some astronomical return on investment. I jumped into the world of creative finance because, frankly, I was broke. I acquired nearly all my properties while I was either self-employed or working for less than $15 per hour. I simply had no choice: be creative or don't invest at all. Along the way, I've made a lot of mistakes, wasted a lot of time, and made more than a few bad investments. However, the many lessons I've learned from it all have made me the investor I am today, so my hope is that I can now share those with you.

All that said, this book is not about me. This book is about **you and your future**, no matter what your past has been or how much money is in your checking account. This book is about giving you the educational tools you need to start investing in real estate, whether you have a million dollars in the bank or six bucks to your name.

It's Not About Being Broke or Irresponsible

I realize that creative real estate investing holds a special appeal for people who absolutely no money in their checking account, but I want to be clear that I don't equate creative real estate investing with having no money. Yes, the two often go together, but that's not what this book is about.

No matter how much money you have in your checking account or IRA, there will always be real estate that you cannot afford.

After all, no matter how much money you have in your bank account or IRA, there will always be real estate that you cannot afford. There is always another level, and getting to that level requires a strong commitment to creative real estate investing. Even the most wealthy and successful real estate investors use a heavy amount of creative finance to continue their business; I would even argue that their skills at buying real estate with no or little money down are what have contributed most to their success.

Therefore this book is for YOU if you are interested in doing more deals, enjoying more cash flow, and increasing your income through creative real estate investing.

This Book Is Not About Getting Rich Quick

Yes, fortunes have been made in real estate, and some of those fortunes have been made rather quickly. However, for the vast majority of real estate investors, this is simply not going to happen, and I am not promising anything different.

This book is about applying creativity as leverage to acquire real estate, and this doesn't happen overnight. Building up a portfolio can take years, and the speed at which that portfolio grows depends heavily on a healthy dose of luck, location, and timing. That said, please don't be discouraged. Creative real estate investing truly is an amazing vocation that can transform your future and the financial destiny of your family forever, and I'm excited to share with you the strategies I've used throughout my career.

To Whom Is This Book For?

There are hundreds of ways to make money in real estate and hundreds of books written about each of the various strategies.[1] Therefore, I think we should discuss *whom* this book is for before we jump headfirst into the content.

This book is for anyone interested in investing in real estate using other people's money. Whatever strategy you expect to use or niche you plan to enter, I believe the lessons in this book can help you find

---

[1] To see the my top choices for real estate investing books, head to
http://www.biggerpockets.com/renewsblog/2013/04/14/best-real-estate-books/

greater success.

Although I am primarily a buy-and-hold real estate investor, interested in the extra monthly income (cash flow) that owning numerous rental properties can provide, and even though I tend to mix in the occasional flip or wholesale deal just to keep things interesting, rental properties are my bread and butter and my area of expertise. That said, the lessons in this book *will* apply for those looking to engage in all types of real estate investing. In fact, Chapter Nine of this book deals exclusively with the concept of real estate wholesaling and finding amazing deals, so be sure to stick around for that.

You CAN Afford It

Each week, Joshua Dorkin (the founder and CEO of BiggerPockets.com) and I have the honor of sitting down with successful real-life real estate investors on the BiggerPockets Podcast and asking them about how they built their business, the successes they've had, the failures they've faced, and more. Perhaps the most popular segment of the show comes at the end, during the "Famous Four"—four questions we ask each and every guest. The first question is simple but powerful: What is your favorite real estate book?

The number one answer given by 80% of our guests thus far has been the same: *Rich Dad Poor Dad: What The Rich Teach Their Kids About Money That the Poor and Middle Class Do Not!* by Robert T. Kiyosaki.

I am amazed by the sheer number of investors out there who credit this one simple book as the inspiration for their investing career, and I'm right there with them. This book was a huge turning point for me and motivated me to start thinking about my financial future in a new light. Although not a textbook for real estate in any way, *Rich Dad Poor Dad* was foundational in the lives of many real estate investors because it changed the mind-set of everyone who read it. Personally, it completely blew my mind wide open with new possibilities and ways of thinking.

Perhaps the greatest mindset–expanding revelation in this book comes when Kiyosaki tells a story about the two men who had a hand in raising him: his real dad and his best friend's dad. Each had a different way of guiding his family financially, which led to the author's dual perspective on financial matters.

In the book, Kiyosaki states, *"Rich dad forbade the words 'I can't afford it.'… Instead, rich dad required his children to say, 'How can I afford it?' His reasoning, the words 'I can't afford it' shut down your brain. It didn't have to think anymore. 'How can I afford it?' opened up the brain. Forced it to think and search for answers."*[2]

I still remember the day I read that; my entire world seemed to turn upside down. I had been raised in a household of "we can or we can't afford that" and so was accustomed to turning my brain off as soon as I reached the point of "no." When I suddenly realized that there was a different way of thinking, something ignited inside me, and my quest for creative finance began.

At that point, I stopped saying, "I can't afford it" and "I can't do it" and began asking, "How can I afford it?" and "How can I do it?" I realized people were making money with real estate investing and were not using any of their own money. I was going to do the same, and I hope this book will help you do so as well.

However, before we go too far down the "let's invest with no

---

[2]Robert T. Kiyosaki and Sharon L. Lechter, *Rich Dad Poor Dad: What the Rich Teach Their Kids About Money That the Poor and Middle Class Do Not!* Warner Books, New York, NY, 1997.

money" road, we need to ask one fundamental question...

Should You Really Invest with No Money Down?

A lot of people out there would advise you not to invest in real estate if you don't have significant financial resources of your own to use as a large down payment. Others, such as popular financial radio talk show host and author Dave Ramsey, have even more strict views and argue that you should *only* invest in real estate if you can pay 100% cash for the property you want.

At the other end of the spectrum are those who would advise you to get into real estate no matter what, however you can. Scam, steal, and squeeze your way in to make a buck. After all, what is important is getting rich as quickly as possible so you can start driving that convertible, lying on that beach, and watching your money grow.

So what's the truth? Should you really try to invest in real estate using creative methods? Should you put this book down immediately and go get a second job working at a fast food joint?

I can only speak for myself and my own risk tolerance, but I believe that a happy medium can be found. I believe all investments are risky to some degree. However, as the great hockey player Wayne Gretzky once said, "You miss 100% of the shots you don't take." In other words, had I not taken that first step toward investing in real estate without any money, I would not be where I am today.

- Have I struggled? Yes!
- Have I lost money? Of course!
- Would I change any of it? Not a chance!

I love the freedom that real estate investing offers, and I was willing to use my creativity in place of the cash needed to get started. I had more time and creativity than money, and I leveraged that into a profitable career—and I wouldn't hesitate to do it again.

If you are someone who advocates being content with a traditional job and saving up for that first cash purchase, more power to you. I wish you well, and I'm fully convinced that's the best route for you to take. However, for me, working 40 years behind a desk so I can be a millionaire when I retire at 65 is hardly a worthy goal.

For me, working 40 years behind a desk so I can be a millionaire when I retire at 65 is hardly a worthy goal.

I want to live today *and* when I retire.

That is what motivated me to start creative real estate investing, and that is what continues to motivate me today. That said, I want to make a few things very clear about creative finance. I like to think of real estate as a game, and as such, certain rules must be followed. I call these the Four Rules of Creative Investing.

The Four Rules of Creative Investing

I like to speed.

Traveling down the freeway, something just seems wrong about going the speed limit. I have to push the limits just a little. This is what intrigues me about the Autobahn in Germany. This federal highway has no federally mandated blanket speed limit, which makes it a dream for people like me.

However, just because the highway has no speed limits, that doesn't mean a driver can afford to be stupid.

In fact, Autobahn drivers are mandated to control their speed during adverse weather conditions and in urban areas of the road. Additionally, an "advisory speed limit" of 81 mph applies to the entire freeway system to protect drivers.

What does this have to do with creative real estate investing? Creativity in real estate is a kind of open road that often appears to be "rule free." However, the same conditions that make it so exhilarating can also lead to the greatest crashes. Therefore, investing in creative real estate has its own "advisory speed limits" in the form of four important guidelines.

These are four of the primary rules and advisory limits of creative real estate investing. These have been passed down from one established investor to another with the goal of keeping aspiring investors from crashing and burning.

1. When investing creatively, you need to find even better deals than those who invest normally. Let me explain what I mean. Let's say a certain home is worth $100,000. A traditional investor might pay $100,000 for that home, put a 30% down payment ($30,000) on the property, and make a nice return on investment from the cash flow (the extra money left after all the expenses are paid).

However, if I were to purchase that same house for $60,000 because I took the extra steps necessary to get a great deal, which of us is in the better position? The traditional investor, who has $30,000 of their cash tied up in their property and no real equity, or me, who has nothing invested but owes less?

Creative investing means you must invest in incredible deals, or it's simply not worth doing.

Because of the deal I obtained, I have far greater potential for profit and for a better return on investment than the normal investor, but less of my cash is at risk because I have no cash invested at all.

However, what if I decided to be just a "normal" investor and pay full price for that $100,000 property, with no money down? Most likely, my mortgage payment would be so high that good cash flow would be out of reach, and I would not have the equity necessary to be able to sell the property. In this case, the "good" investor would be in a better position because they owed only $70,000. Hopefully, you are following my argument here... creative investing means you must invest in incredible deals, or it's simply not worth doing.

There are exceptions to this rule, of course. Sometimes the method of financing can sweeten a deal enough to entice you to jump in. We'll talk more about those strategies later in this book.

2. **When investing creatively, you must be extremely conservative.** I'm not talking politics here; I'm talking about planning for the future. This means assuming the worst when buying property. Take as a given that taxes will go up, your unit will sit vacant for a certain percentage of each year (higher than the average for your area), repairs will be numerous and expensive, and you will need to evict deadbeat tenants. Plan for these costs and only buy property that proves to still be a good deal even after a conservative estimate.

If you want easy, then stick with a job, a sizable down payment, and average returns. There is absolutely nothing wrong with that."

Although the analysis side of the real estate transaction is beyond the scope of this book on creative real estate investing, I encourage you to spend some time on this subject by studying how to analyze an investment property on BiggerPockets. For a video tutorial on exactly how I analyze potential rental properties, check out "How to Analyze Real Estate Investents[3]" Also, in Chapter Nine, I go into significant detail about how to analyze a property, including estimating repairs, so stick around for that.

---

[3] http://www.biggerpockets.com/analyzeinvestments

3. Creative finance requires sacrifice. Remember my definition of creative finance: the ability to *trade* cash for creativity. Notice there is a trade-off involved—one you need to accept. Most of the methods I've used to acquire real estate, I didn't learn from a book. Instead, I discovered the methods at 4:00 a.m. after an eight-hour brainstorming session with my wife, my pen, and my paper, desperately trying to figure out the missing puzzle piece that would enable me to close a deal. This is often the trade. It requires jumping through a lot of mental hoops, numerous conversations with others, and the ability to ask for help. Creative real estate investing is a puzzle that takes real mental (and sometimes physical) effort to put together.

If you want easy, then stick with a job, a sizable down payment, and average returns. There is nothing wrong with that, and I'd have chosen the same if I'd had enough money and income when I started. But I didn't, so I chose creativity. I chose to sacrifice. Will you?

4. Creative finance does not mean investing without a cushion. A wise man and mentor once told me, "You can go broke buying good deals." Even though you need to get killer good deals if you are going to invest with no or little money down, you still need to understand that bad stuff happens. Murphy *will* show up on your doorstep and start knocking. He might even move his whole family in. (If you don't understand the reference, Google "Murphy's Law.")

Therefore, maintaining a financial cushion to deal with problems is imperative. You don't need $50,000 in the bank to buy a small rental house, but you *do* need to be able to weather the storms that will come, relative to the size of the property you are buying and that property's risk for loss.

For example, if you needed to evict a tenant, could you handle several months of lost rent, more than $2,000 in eviction costs, and several thousands of dollars to repair the property? What if you had to do this twice in the same year? These are important questions you must be able to answer, or at least discuss. Many of the strategies in this book will deal with solutions for issues like this, so don't give up on this book quite yet if you are down to your last dollar. These questions do have answers, so hang in there and keep your brain turning.

I can't tell you exactly how much money you'll need to save, because that depends largely on a number of factors, including the following:

1. The strength of your target real estate market
2. Your ability to manage effectively
3. You ability and desire to repair things yourself, if needed
4. How difficult and lengthy evictions are in your state
5. How good your credit is
6. How much cash flow you can get
7. The average purchase price of your target properties
8. The niche you enter
9. The strategy you use
10. And a whole lot more

The point is, be conservative, buy great deals, and have a financial backup plan. If this means spending six months working a second job to save up $5,000 to put into a savings account, then start that second job tomorrow. Maybe it means asking your boss for a raise or lowering your living expenses (remember... sacrifice!). Whatever you need to do, get started as soon as possible. Stop wasting time on excuses and start planning for

Stop wasting time on excuses and start planning for how you are going to get there.

how you are going to get there.

Furthermore, even though having a large financial cushion to weather storms can help you significantly offset risk, you cannot simply throw money at real estate investments and hope they turn out well. Education is key. Will you read the books, study the material, ask the right questions, and insist on becoming the best? I hope so.

No Money Down: A Myth, Scam, or Secret?

I don't really like the phrase "no money down."

Not because the approach is not possible, but because the phrase has been so worn and used by the late-night TV gurus who drive up in their red convertible with two hot bikini-clad babes in the back seat. Big cars, big hair, big promises. "No money down" conveys a sense of "easy money" and a "get rich quick" mentality that is not only flawed and silly – it's dangerous.

As I mentioned earlier, **wealth built through real estate investing is definitely not easy money, nor is it quick**. However, does the widespread overuse of the phrase mean that the concept is impossible to achieve? Does investing in real estate with no money down really work? If you've made it this far into this chapter, you should know that it *is* possible. I've personally done it time and time again, and so have thousands of other, far more successful investors around the world.

Investing in real estate without any money is not a scam or a myth, and it's not a secret that you need thousands of dollars to unlock. It's simply the process of replacing cash needed with the creativity you have. There is a method to the madness of "no money down" real estate, and this book will outline numerous tips for buying property without using your own cash. I and thousands of other investors have used these strategies and tips for years. If you're still not convinced, let me try to make one more thing clear:

Real estate is not free; it requires money. However, when we talk about investing with "no money down," we mean investing with none of *your* money down. In other words, we're talking about using other people's money to buy real estate.

Creative investing is about shifting the source of any needed cash, depending on the strategy. You can do this in numerous ways, and this will all make much more sense as we start examining the different strategies. For now, though, just understand that buying real estate with no money out of pocket (or very little) is a very real and possible thing if you are committed to learning the art. And yes, it is as much an art as it is a science. This book will show you both.

Having the Right Tool for the Right Job

Have you ever hired a handyman to do a job for you?

When a handyman goes to a job site, they don't always know what they are going to need when they get there, so they bring a number of common tools (hammer, saw, drill, etc.) so they'll be prepared for whatever they encounter. If the job requires that something be nailed, they can pull out their hammer. If the job requires a hole to be drilled, they can pull out the drill. A good handyman is prepared with a toolbox full of tools to be able to address whatever is in front of them.

In the same way, a good investor also has a toolbox, and you can fill yours with whichever tools you want. As you work your way through this book, you will learn a number of different strategies. Some of these are relatively easy to understand and apply, while others are high-level concepts that you may need to go over a few times (and just jump into) to fully grasp. Each of these strategies and concepts is a "tool" for your investor toolbox. You may not need each strategy today, and some you may never employ, but by having them all in your toolbox, you will be a more prepared investor—one who can tackle more jobs and will have more success. After all, just like a handyman, the more tools you have, the more projects you can master.

What to Expect in This Book

This book will examine a number of very different strategies for creative finance with real estate investing, but realize that these are only a small fraction of what could be possible when you start using your brain and adopt a "how can I afford it?" mentality. I encourage you to take as many notes as you can so you can revisit the concepts when needed.

Each chapter in this book will cover a different strategy you can use to invest in real estate with little or no money out of pocket. Each chapter will also include a thorough discussion of the risks, downsides, and potential problems involved. Additionally, numerous examples throughout each chapter will help break down the concepts into real-life, actionable plans.

If you have any questions as you work your way through this, I encourage you to visit the BiggerPockets Forums[4] and start asking them there. I can guarantee you that investors are hanging out in the forums right now who have experience in each and every one of the strategies I am about to present, so learn from them by leaning on them! Ask them about their experience, their mistakes, their successes, and fill your toolbox with the highest quality tools you can get.

---

[4] http://www.biggerpockets.com/forums

Will All These Strategies Work for Me?

The short answer is *no*.

Think of this book not as a textbook, but as a piece of literature, one whose lessons can be applied internally but not necessarily used as exact formulas. This book is about learning to think creatively and is filled with stories of individuals who have done exactly this. Your ability to carry out certain strategies will rely heavily on a number of factors, including your location, your personal place in life (family commitments, free time, willingness to sacrifice, etc.), your finances, your personality, and more.

For example, I might mention a rental house that an investor purchased for $120,000. Some of you might scream, "$120,000 for a rental house? That's highway robbery!" while others would shout, "$120,000 for a rental house? That wouldn't buy a parking spot in my area!"

Real estate investing and the strategies for creative finance are heavily defined by location. Does this mean the strategies outlined will not work for your area? Not necessarily. You may be able to tweak a specific strategy to work wonders in your area The point is to open your mind, learn what works in other markets, and train yourself to think creatively and apply those strategies to your own local market.

If you are ready to get started, to open your mind to the possibilities of buying real estate for little or no money down, turn the page, and we'll begin by talking about how I got started: with an *owner-occupied investment property.*

CHAPTER TWO: OWNER-OCCUPIED INVESTMENT PROPERTIES

At first, you might be a little confused.

After all, aren't we supposed to be talking about investing, not buying a personal home? If so, why am I using the term "owner occupied" in this chapter title? I wanted to begin this section by discussing this special kind of real estate investment for two reasons:

1. This is the way I and thousands of other investors started our career.
2. This can be one of the absolute cheapest ways to get started investing in real estate.

This chapter will focus on the strategy of combining your own home with sound investment principles to create a powerful method of getting started without much (or any) cash of your own.

What Exactly Are We Talking About?

First, let's all get on the same page with respect to exactly what we're talking about. An owner-occupied investment property is real estate that has been purchased as an investment but that also doubles as a primary residence for the investor. In other words, the property is both your home *and* an investment property.

Why would you want to do this? Because America loves homeowners! Owning a home is the American dream and ss a result, our society has created some excellent incentives for those who want to buy a home, and when you combine those benefits with the knowledge needed to profit at real estate investing, you can skyrocket your chances for success while lowering the threshold for getting started. For example,

- Homeowners can purchase a home with a mortgage that requires as little as 0% down.
- Homeowners get lower, fixed interest rates.
- Homeowners can qualify with lower credit scores.
- Homeowners are often given the first option to buy foreclosures (especially HUD homes, which are properties that have been foreclosed upon by the U.S. Department of Housing and Urban Development).
- Homeowners can often negotiate better deals with sellers.

We'll go into the specifics on how to do all this later in the chapter, but first let's look at the two primary ways of applying this strategy: a single-family home or a small, multifamily home.

Owner-Occupied Single-Family Home

Let me tell you a tale of two college grads.

Both graduated college with the usual amount of student loan debt, got married, found great jobs paying $5,000 per month, and decided to buy a house for their family.

The first buys a McMansion in the suburbs. The home is everything a family could want: manicured lawn, granite countertops, Brazilian cherry hardwood floors, and more. The family is very happy but spends roughly $2,000 per month just to pay the mortgage—and this is on top of their car payments, student loans, private preschool for their kids, and other middle class bills.

The second college grad buys a house knowing it will not be the family's "final home." They purchase a three-bedroom, two-bath home in a working class neighborhood and put a little sweat equity into painting and landscaping, making it a great house to start out in. The best part? Their total mortgage payment is just $850 per month.

After a year, both college grads, for whatever reason, want to move and decide to rent their home. College grad #1 quickly learns that the most he can get for his home is $1,800 per month in rent. However, his payment is $2,000, not counting maintenance, repairs, and more. He can't sell the house because what he owes is the same as its current value, so by selling, he would actually lose money because he would have to pay the real estate agent and closing costs. College grad #2, however, finds that his home will rent for $1,500, when his payment is only $850, thereby netting him significant extra cash flow each month.

Far too many Americans treat their home as some holy investment, when really, it's putting them in financial hell.

As Kiyosaki explains in *Rich Dad Poor Dad*, buying a single-family home to live in is not an "investment," it's a liability. It costs you money each and every month, takes a significant amount of money to maintain each year, and is probably your single biggest expense. Far too many Americans treat their home as some holy investment, when really, it's putting them in financial hell.

So why do I refer it here as an "investment"? As the story of the two college grads illustrates, you can consider a single-family home an investment if you purchase it with the intention of using it as a real estate investment in the future or if you can build substantial equity[5] by doing some light rehab and then parlay that equity into greater investments later.

On the rental property side, banks generally assume that you will stay in the home for a short time (and sometimes contractually require it), usually a year, but if you move out, you do not need to obtain a new loan. Your loan will stick with the property no matter where you move. Therefore, you can buy a home to live in, move out some time later, and continue to use this home as an investment property. This is how I acquired several of my early properties.

The same principle, as outlined in the story of the two college grads, relates to house flipping and is how I got into real estate at the very beginning.

My No Money Down Beginning

I had just graduated college and was working a barely more than minimum wage job when a friend's sister (who was a real estate agent) told me that for me, buying a house would be cheaper than renting one. I looked into the numbers and discovered she was right.

Although I had no idea what I was doing, I decided to purchase a four-bedroom, one-bath home that, well, was downright ugly. I rented out the bedrooms to some friends (so I could live there for free), slowly fixed the place up, and nine months later, sold the

---

[5] Equity: The difference between how much a property is worth and how much you owe on it.

property for a $20,000 profit. During this time, I used none of my own money but relied on a 100% mortgage to purchase the property and used mostly credit cards to fix it up.

Note: I don't necessarily recommend using credit cards, but doing so did help me bridge the gap I needed to make stuff happen. Although I believe credit cards are exceptionally dangerous, I have a hard time vilifying something that helped me get to where I am. If you plan to use credit cards in your investing plan, be sure to have a rock solid, 100% way of repaying the money quickly, and never borrow more than you can afford to pay the minimum payment on.

While most of my friends were busy playing video games and chasing girls, I was turning thin air into a $20,000 profit and was ultimately able to pay for a dream wedding and honeymoon with my new wife. Yes, I could have purchased a beautiful home that needed no work, but instead I chose to buy something that could double as both an investment and a primary residence—and it paid off well for me.

Purchasing a small multifamily property can have a tremendous impact on your financial future, especially when combined with the power of being an owner occupant.

Could you do the same? You tell me! This is just one simple example, but the possibilities are endless when you use your head and start thinking creatively.

Let's move on to another popular form of an owner-occupied investment: the small multifamily home.

Owner-Occupied Multifamily Homes

Chances are good that you've rented a unit in one of these places in the past or you know someone who has. They exist in every market, in every neighborhood, and at every price point, and purchasing a small multifamily property can have a tremendous impact on your financial future, especially when combined with the power of being an owner occupant.

A small multifamily property is a 2-4 unit residential property, so an owner-occupied multifamily property is one where the owner lives in one of the units.

The neat part is this: duplexes, triplexes, and fourplexes are all considered "residential," so if you live in one of the units, even for a short time, the American benefits to home ownership are no different than what I outlined earlier. In other words, most banks view small multifamily properties exactly the same as single-family homes. This is good news for you!

(Keep in mind, once a property reaches five units, you enter a whole new ball game of "commercial real estate," which is ineligible for the benefits related to owner-occupied properties that we are talking about here. There are still ways to buy properties with five or more units without using your own cash, but this chapter on owner-occupied investments won't explain those techniques. We'll cover them in later chapters instead.)

Because 2-4 unit properties are considered residential, they come with low rates, easy(ish) financing, and a smaller down payment required. Additionally, when you buy smart and get a great deal, you might be able to live for free and get paid for doing so.

When you purchase a great small multifamily deal, the rent your tenants pay each month can cover all the property's expenses—and more. For example, if you buy a fourplex, live in one unit, and rent each of the other units for $500 per month, you could be making $1,500 per month in income. If your loan, taxes, insurance, utilities, and other expenses total just $1,200, you could essentially be getting paid $300 a month just to live in the home.

Even better, when the time comes to move out and into your future home, you can rent that fourth unit for even more income. Let me break these numbers down again in an easier-to-understand table:

Total Monthly Rental Income	$1,500 ($500 x 3)
Total Monthly Expenses*	$1,200
Cash Flow	$300

Expenses include an average of *all* possible expenses, such as the mortgage payment, property taxes, insurance, flood insurance (if needed), property management, utilities, repairs, capital expenditures (the big items you'll need to save up for, like a new roof, appliances, etc.), and any other costs that might come up. To help estimate these expenses, be sure to check out the article "How to Estimate Expenses on a Rental Property."[6]

Again, the success of your owner-occupied multifamily home depends almost entirely on your ability to find a great deal, so don't skip that part of your education. There are numerous great resouces across the BiggerPockets website that can help you learn how to find great deals, and in chapter nine of this book we'll spend a lot of time on the subject as well. Study up on the best methods for finding and analyzing properties so you'll recognize a good deal when you see one.

---

[6] http://www.biggerpockets.com/estimateexpenses

Single-Family or Multifamily?

Whether you plan to buy a single-family home and turn it into an investment someday or buy a small multifamily property to use as an investment property right now, you can see how important this stage of your investment career can be.

The choice is yours as to which type of property to buy: single family or multifamily. In many ways, the decision comes down to your position in life. Do you have a large family? If so, you may want to focus on a single-family property. Are single-family homes too expensive in your area? If so, you may want to focus on a small, multifamily property instead.

Obviously, investing in an owner-occupied single-family home is more about appreciation than cash flow, and because I'm a cash flow investor, I am pretty strongly in favor of the multifamily idea. However, once again, it all comes down to your lifestyle.

Why Buy an Owner-Occupied Investment?

What does any of this have to do with creative finance and buying real estate for little or no money down? After all, buying these properties takes money, doesn't it?

Yes, but likely not as much as you think.

The fact is, there are low money down lending opportunities that exist for homeowners that simply do not exist for the typical real estate investor. By taking advantage of these opportunities, you can start building your rental portfolio with very little out-of-pocket cash and get started sooner than you may have imagined.

The rest of this chapter will deal with the "creative" side of buying an owner-occupied investment property. We'll explore how you can get into a home for less money than you think and consider a few specific loan products you can use to get into your first property.

However, before we begin discussing those techniques, let's quickly address one important fundamental question...

Should You Even Buy a Home?

When I bought my first house, I took a hammer and smashed a hole in the wall—just because I could. You see, buying my first home was exciting because it was mine. I could do what I wanted, when I wanted, and no landlord could tell me "no." For me, owning a home is one of the greatest feelings on earth. However, buying a home is not for everyone.

If you are flat broke, up to your eyelids in debt, switching jobs often, and can't seem to resist calling those late-night infomercial numbers for crap you can't afford, maybe you should focus on getting your life and budget in order first. Or if the average home price is $995,000 where you live and you can't move to a lower cost area, buying a home might not be the right move just now (unless you can find a screaming good deal). Or, if you have a 550 credit score because of some past mistakes, buying a home simply might need to wait until you can qualify.

Investing in real estate by purchasing a home is not a lighthearted, flippant decision. It requires a plan, stability, and moderately good credit. However, I also believe that buying a home is not meant just for boring old folks who have 2.1 kids, a dog, and a career at a Fortune 500 company. If you have decent credit, a stable job, and a modest balance in your savings, you can enter the world of homeownership. What's more, if you are smart about it, you can simultaneously enter the world of real estate investing and live for cheap or free while getting firsthand, on-the-job training to be a landlord.

Now, let's move on to specifics. The programs outlined in the following sections are the ones used most often by owner-occupied investors to obtain properties with no or little money down. (Keep in mind that I am not a mortgage professional. Loan requirements and details change often, so always check with a qualified mortgage professional before moving forward with any of this information.)

FHA Insured Loans

One of the most popular methods of buying a home today, especially for low or middle class borrowers, is through the use of an Federal Housing Authority insured loan, generally just referred to as an FHA loan. The Federal Housing Authority is a United States Federal agency under the Department of Housing and Urban Development (HUD) that performs a number of housing and mortgage related activities to encourage home ownership and market stability.

Before the late 2007 real estate crash, FHA loans were mostly ignored because anyone with a pulse seemed to be able to qualify for a mortgage using no or little money down. (Remember the story I told earlier of my first live-in flip? Yep, I was able to pay no money down as a college grad with a low-paying job. Don't expect that anymore!) In fact, in 2005, less than 5% of purchases used an FHA loan, but FHA market share reached 28.1% of all purchases in 2009, during the height of the mortgage crisis.[7]

The term "FHA loan" is a bit of a misnomer, though, because the FHA does not, in fact, provide loans. Instead, it simply insures the loan against loss. In other words, the U.S. Government tells the banks (please read the following in a New Jersey mobster accent),

"Look, fellas, we know these people don't have enough of a down payment to

---

[7] Source: FHA-Insured Single-Family Mortgage Originations Market Share Report: 2013 – Q3.

get a regular loan from yous guys. So, I'll tell you what we're gonna do. You scratch our back, we'll scratch yours. Go ahead and offer the loan anyway, and good ole Uncle Sam will make sure you're taken care of should something bad happen and the homeowners stop paying."

FHA Loan Specifics

To offset the risk the government takes when insuring these loans, the FHA passes some additional costs on to the borrowers through the use of two special fees (when the loan-to-value[8] is greater than 78%). These fees are known as the Mortgage Insurance Premium (MIP) and must be used in your calculations when considering using an FHA loan for a property. The MIP is charged both upfront, in the form of a one-time fee that is usually wrapped into the loan, and monthly, in the form of a monthly fee that is added to your loan. Both fees are based on a percentage of the purchase price and typically result in an extra 1%–2% fee up front and an additional monthly fee of roughly $100 per month for each $100,000 financed.

FHA loans stand out in the lending world because of their extremely low down payment requirements- just 3.5% of the purchase price at the time of this writing. This means an individual could use an FHA loan to purchase a single-family home or small multifamily property with considerably less than the 20% down payment normally required, as long as they plan to initially live in the property. This makes the FHA loan very attractive to first-time homebuyers and first-time investors.

Let's look at a quick example of how you might use an FHA loan to get started investing in real estate.

---

[8] Loan to Value (LTV): The ratio of the mortgage amount to the total appraised worth of a property. For example, a home with an $80,000 mortgage that is worth $100,000 would have an 80% LTV.

Lindsay found a triplex in a good neighborhood listed for $100,000 that currently brings in $500 per month, per unit, in income. She is able to negotiate with the seller a purchase price of $90,000 for the property, and they will pay $2,700 toward her closing costs, which covers about half her costs. Lindsay then uses an FHA loan to get a mortgage on the property, needing to put down 3.5% of the $90,000 ($3,150 down) plus another $2,700 in miscellaneous loan fees and prepaid insurance/tax amounts.

Lindsay's monthly mortgage payment is approximately $530, including the MIP we discussed earlier, plus $150 for taxes and insurance, for a total payment of $680 per month. She rents the other two units out for a total of $1,000 per month and manages the property herself, collecting the difference in cash flow each month (after paying expenses and saving for maintenance issues). After several years, Lindsay moves on to buy her dream house, renting out the unit she had been living in and getting even more cash flow while building her wealth automatically.

Risks and Drawbacks to the FHA Loan

While the FHA loan program seems to be a great one (and it can be), you should be aware of some major issues and drawbacks before jumping into an FHA deal. I do not want to scare you away from these loans, but I feel that understanding all risks and dangers before engaging in any real estate investment is vitally important.

1. MIP – As mentioned earlier, the Mortgage Insurance Premium can be a real cash flow killer, so be sure to only buy amazing deals when using the FHA loan to purchase property. In the example of

Lindsay and the triplex I used earlier, Lindsay would have almost $1,200 per year extra if her loan had not included that MIP.

2. One Time Use Only – For those of you who are thinking, "Great! I'll use this FHA trick every year and get a dozen properties in the next 12 years," I have some bad news: the FHA allows you to have only one FHA loan in your name at a time. Bummer. However, if you have sufficient equity in your property and the credit/income to justify it, you can refinance[9] your loan into a conventional (normal) mortgage and pursue another FHA loan.

3. Red Tape – Additionally, dealing with the government in any way always seems to involve more hassle, more red tape, and more waiting than dealing with private banks. Once you have the loan, it might be great, but actually getting the loan might take a little extra fancy footwork.

Summary of the FHA Loan

Should you use the FHA loan? Obviously, every situation is different, but I am a strong proponent of using this kind of loan when the deal makes sense. The FHA loan is ideal for first-time real estate investors and those who have minimal cash but decent credit and job stability. Although it isn't a technique to obtain real estate for *no* money down, it can get you pretty darn close with just a 3.5% down payment plus closing costs, which is doable for most people, even if you have to save up for a few months.

I believe the FHA loan, when used correctly, can be a powerful tool for new investors to acquire their first deal with minimal cash out of pocket. Again, the MIP and low down payment requirements demand that you get an even better deal than the typical homeowner (this is a running theme in this book, in case you hadn't noticed), so

---

[9] Refinancing: Obtaining a new loan to pay off a previous one.

shop around, be selective, and claim a great property.

Most banks and lending institutions offer FHA-insured loans, so ask your mortgage professional about your options, and be sure to look into any policy changes since the publishing of this book.

The 203k Loan

This next loan I'm going to talk about gets me real excited because of the potential it has in helping new investors get started building serious equity without a lot of cash out of pocket. After reading about the FHA loan just moments ago, this should be fairly easy to comprehend. Let's get into it!

One of the subsets of the FHA loan is called a 203k loan, so named because it's based on section 203(k) of the National Housing Act from the Department of Housing and Urban Development (we'll stick with calling it the 203k loan).

Although the 203k loan is part of the FHA-insured loan program, and thus adheres to the main rules and requirements already discussed, I decided to dedicate a separate section of this chapter to this loan because of some major benefits it offers and the power it can have for a real estate investor looking to maximize their live-in investments.

At its core, the 203k loan is a two-part loan that includes funds to both purchase *and* rehab a home to the specifics you desire. In other words, you can buy a property that is in desperate need of new paint, carpet, smell removal, or other cosmetic (or structural) attention, and the 203k loan allows you to roll all those costs into the loan, so you don't need to pay for them out of pocket.

For example, let's go back to the story I shared earlier about the normal FHA loan, Lindsay, and the $90,000 triplex. Let's say that the triplex had just gone through foreclosure and was in desperate need of some new interior paint, carpet, and cabinets. Normally, getting a bank to even lend on a property in such a condition might be impossible, but with the 203k loan, Lindsay can make this work.

After her offer is accepted, during the due diligence period, Lindsay hires an FHA-approved contractor (recommended to her by her lender) to give her a bid on the repairs needed. It comes in at $10,000. Lindsay's purchase price on the property was $90,000, so the total cost of the project ends up being $100,000. This is the number on which the FHA bases it 3.5% down payment requirement, so Lindsay must pay just $3,500 down plus part of the closing costs to buy the property. After the property sale closes and Lindsay takes possession of the home, the FHA-approved contractor goes in and replaces the carpet, paints the interior, and adds the new kitchen cabinets. The FHA then inspects the property to make sure the work was done correctly, and it pays the contractor directly.

Lindsay was able to secure the now-rehabbed triplex for less than $5,000 out of pocket and will make that money back from the cash flow the property will generate in less than a year.

As you can probably see, the 203k loan holds tremendous potential for a smart investor. Adding value to a property through rehabbing is one of the fastest ways to build wealth quickly, and here the government is willing to lend you money to pay for those repairs!

The 203k loan allows you to avoid the competition for already beautiful homes and instead focus on properties that most other homebuyers are too afraid to consider. Rather than offering $90,000 on the triplex in our triplex example, could Lindsay have offered

$80,000? $70,000? $60,000? Those discounts are not outside the realm of possibility when one is dealing with distressed properties, and it's one of the reasons I personally focus almost entirely on properties where I can get great deals and "force" the value higher through rehabs. Let's look at another example of how you could use a 203k loan to invest in real estate with little money out of pocket.

Eddie lives in an expensive part of Boston where the cost of a single-family home is far beyond his comfort level, with prices ranging from $400,000 to $600,000 for a nice home. This translates to $2,000–$3,000 per month for a mortgage payment, not including any expenses.

However, Eddie finds a vacant duplex that has recently been foreclosed on by a national bank, and the place is trashed. Eddie and his contractor estimate that to completely clean up and renovate the property would cost approximately $34,000. So Eddie makes an offer on the duplex for $315,000, and after some negotiations, the sellers accept his offer.

After all the closing costs and other charges are added into the equation, Eddie is required to bring about $12,000 to the closing table. He gets a loan for $349,000, which covers the agreed-upon purchase price, plus the $34,000 needed for repairs. After all is said and done, his mortgage payment is $2,600 per month with taxes and insurance, and he rents out one-half of the duplex for $2,900, leaving extra money each month to save up for repairs, maintenance, and more. In two years, Eddie moves out and rents his unit out for $2,900 per month as well, making *huge* cash flow each and every month.

Additionally, after the repairs are finished, Eddie has the property reappraised and finds it is worth nearly $500,000, meaning Eddie has built up $150,000 in equity. Not a bad way to start.

203k Loan Specifics

There are actually two types of 203k loans, depending on the type of work you plan on doing:

- the 203k
- the 203k *streamline*

The difference lies in the extent of the rehab involved. The 203k streamline loan can be used for smaller cosmetic problems, like painting, carpet, and smells, while the regular 203k loan can be used for structural changes, like moving walls or building additions. Contractors that work on the property rehab must be FHA approved. However, most licensed/bonded contractors can become FHA approved by simply submitting the correct paperwork to the bank, and your mortgage professional can help them do this.

Also, at the time of this writing, FHA-approved contractors are required to do the work only if the total cost of renovations exceeds $15,000, so if the property just needs some basic repairs that you can and will do yourself, you can save even more. Finally, all work on a property purchased with a 203k loan must be completed within six months of the loan's closing, though lenders do reserve the right to shorten this time line.

Risks and Drawbacks to the 203k Loan

As with any loan, the 203k loan has both benefits and pitfalls. We've already mentioned some of the downsides of using an FHA loan, and because this product is also part of the FHA program, the same dangers exist. However, you need to note some additional concerns before you venture out to buy a property with a 203k loan.

1. Even More Red Tape – Speaking from experience, I can tell you that the 203k loan involves even more red tape than the regular FHA loan, so be prepared for a paperwork mess, mainly because there are many more moving parts in the machine (contractors, lenders, reimbursements, etc.).

This can also affect the speed of the lending process, so be sure to give yourself ample time to close when making an offer on a property for which you'll be using a 203k loan. Also, I recommend finding a great mortgage professional who specializes in the 203k loan program to help you navigate these cumbersome waters. These experts can be difficult to find, given that most mortgage professionals have never done or cannot do a 203k loan, so make a lot of phone calls and interview to find the best!

2. Rehabs Are Risky Business – If you've ever been involved in a rehab, you already know that it can be a significant undertaking with numerous risks and dangers. Besides trying to manage contractors and deal with the drama that accompanies any rehab, you'll have to deal with the potential that something could go wrong on the project that would require more money than you had anticipated spending, and HUD won't cover those items. For example, if your contractor opens up the walls and discovers bad wiring, you may be forced to cover the cost of this change out of pocket.

3. MIP – Again, because the 203k loan is part of the FHA program, you'll be required to pay the up-front MIP, as well as the monthly MIP payment, if the loan to value ratio is greater than 78%. This can add hundreds of dollars to your monthly payment, depending on the size of the loan. Therefore, if you are investing for monthly cash flow, be sure to consider the MIP payment when running your numbers.

Summary of the 203k Loan

I truly believe that when used correctly, the 203k loan might just be the most perfect loan product for a new investor trying to break into the investing game. The key, however, is in the phrase "when used correctly."

The ideal scenario is finding a property with basic cosmetic issues—like peeling paint, old carpet, and bad smells—that can be acquired for far below value and with significant potential for cash flow or quick appreciation after purchase. Whether the house in question is a single-family or multifamily (two to four units) property, use the 203k loan to add immediate benefit with minimal out of pocket expenses.

The VA Loan

Another popular loan option for many homebuyers is the VA loan. This loan product was created by the U.S. Department of Veterans Affairs and operates in a very similar fashion to the FHA-insured loan—with a few notable differences.

1. VA loans are designed exclusively for U.S. military service members, veterans, and eligible surviving spouses.
2. VA loans can be funded with **no money down**. No, that's not a typo—you can really get a home for zero down.
3. Unlike the FHA loans, VA loans require no private mortgage insurance, meaning your payment will be lower than if you used an FHA loan.
4. The VA loan allows the seller to pay 100% of the buyer's closing costs, unlike the FHA loans, which limits the seller to just 3%. This means a VA loan can truly be 100% no money down.

Like the FHA loans, the VA loan is an "insured" loan that the government provides to protect the majority of the lender's capital in case the borrower defaults. Also, like the FHA and other residential loans, a VA loan can be used to purchase single-family homes or small multifamily properties with up to four units, but only for individuals purchasing a primary residence.

I won't go into a lot of detail on using a VA loan to invest in real estate, because the principles are almost identical to those of the FHA loan, and any differences can be explained to you by your VA lender.[10] However, for more information on VA loans and investing while serving in the military, be sure to check out our article "Investing in American Real Estate While Serving in the US Military."[11]

USDA Loans

Though it is perhaps the least well-known of the government-insured loan programs, the U,S. Department of Agriculture offers one that works very similarly to the FHA and VA loan programs.

Now, you are probably thinking, "Isn't that the same government department that certifies my hamburger meat?"

Yep!

Although commonly referred to as simply the "USDA loan," the full name of the program we'll be primarily discussing here is the USDA Rural Development Single Family Housing Guaranteed Loan Program (though the USDA does offer several different loan programs from which to choose). You can see why "USDA loan" is much easier to say.

---

[10] If you are a member (former or active) of a U.S. military service or a family member of one, learn more about VA loans by visiting Benefits.va.gov.

[11] http://www.biggerpockets.com/renewsblog/2014/01/29/investing-american-real-estate-serving-us-military/

USDA Loan Specifics

The USDA loan is similar to the other programs we've discussed already (the FHA, 203k, and VA loans), but in many ways takes the benefits from each and combines them into a really great loan product, which includes the following advantages:

- 100% loan financing
- No monthly private mortgage insurance (an added monthly charge for low-down payment mortgages) or MIP (as seen with the FHA Loan)
- No maximum purchase price
- Certain repairs and upgrades can be financed into the loan
- Seller can pay up to 6% toward the buyer's closing costs

In other words, the USDA loan includes a lot of really great features than can help you get into a home with almost nothing out of pocket. So why doesn't everyone do a USDA loan?

Just as the VA loan is only for veterans, the USDA loan has a strict qualifier as well: **rural single family homes only**, for low- to moderate-income homebuyers. But what exactly is "rural" and what qualifies as "low to moderate income"? You might actually be surprised, and chances are good that you could qualify for a USDA loan if you live outside a major city by any small distance—you don't need to live 500 miles into the desert or deep in the Midwest farmland.

To check your eligibility for location, the USDA actually has a nice map feature you can use to check your status on their website.[12]

---

[12] http://eligibility.sc.egov.usda.gov/eligibility/welcomeAction.do

As for income eligibility, the USDA loan requirements change depending on the county in which you live, but if your household income hovers near the average income of most Americans, there is a good chance you do qualify. To qualify currently, your income can't exceed 115% of the median income for the area in which the property is listed. For example, in my county, the threshold is $75,000 per year.

Risks and Drawbacks to the USDA Loan

Let's look at a few of the specific negative characteristics of the USDA loan so you'll have a better understanding of whether you can use it.

1. **Location Specific** – Perhaps the biggest drawback of the USDA loan is that many homes, because of their location, simply will not qualify, though a surprising number still will. Be sure to check the USDA website to determine if your location would qualify for a USDA loan.

2. **More Red Tape and Waiting** – Just like the other loan programs we've discussed thus far, you may have to deal with significant waiting, red tape, and other obnoxious paper problems when obtaining a USDA loan. I sold a home recently to a woman who used a USDA loan, and the loan took nearly four months to close because of a "backlog" at the USDA. Be prepared for possibilities like this.

3. **Single Family Only** – As the name of the loan would suggest, the USDA loan is eligible for use only on single-family homes, which means small multifamily properties such as duplexes, triplexes, and fourplexes are out of consideration. With that said, the USDA does offer a 10%

down payment loan on multifamily properties in rural areas (for non-owner occupants). If you want more information on the Guaranteed Rural Rental Housing Program, visit USDA.gov.

4. **High Leverage** – Obtaining a 0% down payment loan requires leveraging yourself to an exceptionally high degree, which could be a negative for some. We've talked about this numerous times already, but leverage is not necessarily a bad thing if the deal is good enough. However, a 100% loan on a mediocre deal may result in a bad deal. Use caution any time you use a highly leveraged loan.

Wrapping It All Up: Owner-Occupied Investment Properties

Being an owner-occupied investor can be a great way to jumpstart your real estate investing future and give you a solid foundation upon which to build your wealth. It's the way thousands of other real estate investors have started, because it can be done with little to no money out of pocket.

Let me emphasize this one final time: the key to a successful owner-occupied investment strategy is getting a great deal, something that can serve as a great buy and hold investment for the future or can gain you significant equity right off the bat.

The key to a successful owner-occupied investment strategy is getting a great deal.

If you are interested in buying your first owner-occupied investment, I recommend reading through the rest of this book to get a solid grasp on what makes a great deal, and applying that to your home shopping. You may need to be more selective, and the process may take longer than it would take the average homebuyer, but if done correctly, the results could be amazing and set you on a path toward financial success.

Owner-occupied investments can be one of the easiest and most streamlined ways to start your real estate investing journey for little to no money down. As I mentioned earlier, this is the way I started my investing career, and I recommend that most people do the same, because you can gain significant education through "on the job" training and hopefully build up some serious equity or cash flow in the process.

The biggest drawback to owner-occupied investment properties is that you have to live in the property. This is a deal killer for many people who for numerous reasons cannot move or buy their own home. Perhaps they own their dream home already or don't have the credit to qualify for a mortgage. This is okay. This is only one chapter out of ten!

The rest of this book will deal with strategies outside the owner-occupied realm and dig into techniques you can use without needing to live in the investment. Let's move on and look at some other ways you can get involved with real estate investing creatively and without a lot of cash. We'll begin with one of my favorites: *partnerships.*

CHAPTER THREE: PARTNERSHIPS

I'm a huge fan of superhero movies.

You know the type: big Hollywood budget, star-studded cast, and over-the-top special effects, and judging by the recent success of these films, I'm not the only one who loves them. People connect with these films in a unique way, largely because of the connection we feel to the powerful yet emotionally damaged superheroes.

No matter how cool or super these heroes are, they all have one thing in common: partners. Whether that partner is another superhero, a beautiful woman, a government agent, or a wise butler, clearly, even superheroes need a partner.

Why? Because everyone has weaknesses. Yes, even you. No matter how smart, talented, rich, good looking, strong, or wise you are, you still have needs that can be better met by someone else. Partners can compensate for those weaknesses in a powerful way. When investing in real estate, your greatest weakness may be your lack of cash, but you may excel in other areas like

- having knowledge
- being creative
- having flexible time
- the ability to do your own labor
- having a deal or the ability to find one

As a result, using partners to invest in real estate can be a powerful way to move forward without a lot of cash. This chapter covers the concept of partnerships extensively and explains a few strategies for using partners to creatively invest in real estate without a significant amount of money out of pocket.

I hope this chapter will open your eyes to the possibilities partners can bring to your real estate deals. Whether you have done zero deals or 100, I believe the information in this chapter will help you invest in more real estate, build more wealth, and have more fun doing it.

Although I will share several specific techniques and strategies for investing in real estate using partners, recognize that these are not the *only* ways to invest with partners—just a few strategies I've used. As I've mentioned, the purpose of this book is to get your mind thinking creatively, so let's get creative with partners...

Let Me Introduce You to "Bob"

Bob is responsible. Bob pays his bills. Bob has a good job, good credit, a pretty wife, and a nice smile—and he smells terrific. Bob is a banker's best friend. Bob also has some extra cash lying around. There's only one problem: Bob is not a real estate investor.

Bob doesn't find deals, Bob doesn't read the books, Bob doesn't hang out on BiggerPockets.com, and Bob doesn't even know the difference between a lease option and seller financing! (Don't worry; we'll get to both of those later in this book.)

You, on the other hand, find the deals, read the books, hang out on BiggerPockets.com, and can tell the difference between lease options and seller financing (or at least, you will soon). Together, you and Bob could form a superhero team that could take on Batman and Robin—and dominate (at least in Monopoly).

Why Bob?

Let's face it, real estate investing is cool. If the world were a junior high school playground, investors would be the kids with the Air Jordans. Every kid wants to be cool, and every adult wants the same. Although the classification of what's cool may have changed over the years, the basic concept remains the same. Everyone wants to be cool.

Even "Bob."

Bob looks at you, the investor (or soon-to-be investor), and sees "cool." He sees that you are out there, wheeling and dealing, making things happen. You are going places. You are fighting "the man" and building some serious wealth in the process.

Bob wants to be cool, but he does not have the time. Bob wants to invest in real estate, to see his money making money, but he simply cannot. Or will not. By joining forces, you and Bob can become unstoppable.

How Do You Find Bob?

Bob is everywhere. Chances are, many of your family members and friends are "Bobs." Many of the people you run into at the grocery store are "Bobs." Your doctor might be a "Bob."

Now before you run out and ask all your family members and friends for money, wait to hear what I have to say next. I don't actually recommend ever directly asking your Bob for money—at least not at first. After all, when you go to the grocery store, you don't see the cashiers begging for cash, yet your money still ends up in their registers.

Why is this?

Because you trust the store; you trust its brand. Additionally, the store has something you want. It is known for carrying the kinds of products that satisfy your needs, and as a result, you will willingly hand over your hard-earned money.

The same is true when you are raising money for real estate. Developing yourself as a recognizable brand is the number one way to attract money to yourself and your business. I'm not suggesting a national brand (like Coca-Cola or Starbucks) but rather a brand within your community and network.

Building Your Brand

Your brand consists of two parts: yourself and your product. They are two sides of the same coin, and you need both to develop your real estate brand. For example, you might buy Oreo cookies because you trust and like the name Oreo, but also because you were in the mood for a sugary chocolate cookie. Obviously, both parts played a role in your choosing to purchase Oreos. The same applies with your real estate investing. You must develop a brand for yourself personally, as well as for the product you are offering.

Let's dive into this topic a little deeper and separate these two halves so we can look at each one individually.

46

1. Your Personal Brand

The first half of your "brand" involves *you*, the potential investor. What do people immediately think when they see you and talk with you? Do you portray confidence, intelligence, trust?

I believe your personal brand is developed in three primary areas: **reputation**, **knowledge**, and **experience**. Let's talk about each of these, one at a time.

Reputation – Your reputation is a fragile extension of yourself that must be handled with care at all times, one that extends far beyond just your business life.

- Do you do what you say you'll do?
- Do people know you as honest?
- Do you go out of your way to help others?
- How do you treat your family and friends in public?
- What does your Facebook wall say about you?
- What do your clothes say about you?
- What does your choice in friends say about you?
- What does your appearance say about you?
- What does your car say about you?

Your reputation extends to every area of your life, and when you're building a creative real estate business, it matters. I'm not suggesting you dump your wardrobe and your Prius in exchange for an Armani suit and a limo. However, recognize that with every move you make, people are watching. They are looking for someone to look up to, respect, invest with, and partner with. Start building

Your reputation extends to every area of your life, and when you're building a creative real estate business, it matters.

47

your reputation right now as someone who is serious about success.

Knowledge – Secondly, your personal brand is developed through knowledge. I'm sure you know someone in your life who talks a big game but clearly doesn't know what they are talking about half the time. (Admit it, you are thinking about someone right now.) People can smell "that guy" coming from a mile away.

Never pretend to know more than you do, but use your gaps in knowledge as motivation to grow. Don't be afraid to say, "I don't know the answer to that question, but let me get back to you on it."

Knowledge can be gained in various ways, and with this book, you are using one of the best methods: reading. You can also attend real estate meet-ups, sit down with local real estate investors for coffee, listen to real estate podcasts, get involved in online forums, or work (or volunteer) under an experienced real estate investor.

Experience – Finally, your personal brand is strengthened through your experience. Perhaps the most difficult to build for new investors, your track record is your greatest ally in establishing your personal brand. What have you done that will help people trust you?

If you are experienced with real estate or business, this should speak for itself. However, if you are just getting started in this field, building your experience without ever doing a deal is not impossible. Experience can be gained through close proximity to other investors or can be conveyed by a large dose of education and a good reputation. In other words, if you lack experience, strengthen your knowledge and reputation to compensate, and you'll be fine.

2. Your Product

The other side of the "branding coin" is your *product*. It has to be good, and it has to be worth selling. Nabisco did not become the monster company it is because Oreos tasted bad. No, Oreos are probably the best-tasting treat ever invented on planet Earth. (Feel free to disagree, but deep down, we both know I'm right!)

Your real estate deals need to be the same—incredible. If you are having difficulty financing a deal, you need to ask yourself "is this *really* a good deal?"

If people are going to trust your brand, they have to trust the quality and profitability of the product you represent.

Although this is beyond the scope of this book, you really need to have a solid grasp on the math behind real estate investing. Do you truly know what makes a deal a deal, or are you just throwing out wild numbers and hoping for the best? If people are going to trust your brand, they have to trust the quality and profitability of the product you represent.

Additionally, and just as important, you need to present your deals in a manner that reflects their strengths. In other words, presentation matters! When you talk about a deal, do you mention how great you hope it will be, or do you have a three-page written, detailed analysis packet, complete with repair estimates, color photos, and recent sales comps to justify your claims?

(For more information on producing high-quality documents to showcase your deals, check out the BiggerPockets Investment Calculators,[13] which will allow you to run the numbers and analyze deals. You can also print white-label reports to give to potential partners, lenders, investors, and buyers.)

Building Your Brand Will Help You Succeed

---

[13] http://www.biggerpockets.com/calc

If you build yourself into a trustworthy brand, the money will follow. When real estate investing becomes your passion, you will

If you build yourself into a trustworthy brand, the money will follow.

find that you can't help but talk to everyone about it. In turn, the people you talk to about it will talk to their friends about you. Brand loyalty can spread like wildfire if you proactively fan the flame. So what does brand building have to do with partners?

Remember Bob? When you build your brand and develop both sides of the coin, you won't need to go searching for Bob. Bob will find you—and when he does, it'll be time to make him cool.

How to Work with Bob: Four Strategies

Perhaps a neighbor overheard you talking about a recent deal, or your sister's boyfriend's aunt's doctor heard about your skills and wants to get involved. There are many ways I work with Bob to benefit us both, and the type of business relationship you have with your Bob will depend significantly on the case-by-case situation you are in. That said, here are four ways I've worked with Bob to build a mutually beneficial relationship:

1. **Full Equity Partnership** – The first strategy is an equity partnership in which Bob funds the deal using his cash. In this scenario, Bob funds the purchase and the repairs needed, in exchange for a certain split. This works especially well for house flippers. Bob can fund the entire purchase and repair amount while you manage the rehab, and in the end, you split everything 50/50. Mike Simmons explains how he uses this strategy to flip houses with no money of his own on Episode 50 of the BiggerPockets podcast.[14] Let's look at an example.

---

[14] http://www.biggerpockets.com/show50

Real estate investor Cheryl really wants to purchase, rehab, and sell a certain three-bedroom, two-bath townhouse, but she has none of the $250,000 the sellers are asking for the property. She knows that with $50,000 worth of work, she could sell the property for $400,000, so she is eager to put the deal together. She decides to get creative. Cheryl meets with her local real estate mentor, John, and shows him the full deal. He's impressed by the due diligence she's put into it and the solid deal that she presents. Bob agrees to become an full equity partner of Cheryl's, agreeing to fund the entire purchase price and the repairs in exchange for 50% of the profits at the end. John pays for 100% of the expenses and holding costs while Cheryl diligently manages the rehab. After 90 days, the home is sold for $400,000, and Cheryl and John split the profit 50/50. Cheryl clears $35,000 herself after paying the closing costs and fees—with not a penny out of her pocket.

2. Down Payment Equity Partnership – Although many "Bobs" have hundreds of thousands of dollars in the bank, not all potential partners will. However, you can still use Bob to invest with none of your own cash, even if Bob can't come up with the whole purchase price and repairs.

In a Down Payment Equity Partnership, Bob funds the down payment needed, typically 20%–30%. Bob gets the entire mortgage in his name alone (or you can get it in both names, if you prefer), but the legal title is in both names (although most lenders do allow this, yours may not, so always check with your banker). You divide the cash flow and/or equity in whatever split you agree upon. I like 50/50, but as in any partnership, it all comes down to what you negotiate.

> Brian, a relatively new investor, located a triplex in his neighborhood listed at $120,000. He knows the property will make an excellent rental but has no cash to purchase the property. Brian knows he needs a 25% down payment plus about $10,000 to cover minor repairs and closing costs to make the deal come together.
>
> Thinking creatively, Brian talks with Samantha, his aunt, who has been interested in investing in real estate for some time but has been too busy with her day job to jump in. Samantha agrees to pay the $40,000 needed to purchase the triplex and gets the loan for the property in her name, but both Brian and Samantha put their names on the property's title. They obtain a mortgage for $90,000, and all the monthly expenses (mortgage, utilities, management, vacancy, capital expenditures, repairs, etc.) come to $1,400 per month. The triplex is rented for $2,400 per month, so each month, the two make around $1,000 in positive cash flow, which they split 50/50.
>
> Someday, when they sell, they'll split the proceeds 50/50 as well and trade up to a larger deal together. Brian was able to generate $500 per month using no money of his own, just creativity.

3. **Private Lending Partnership** – In this strategy, you offer Bob a solid interest rate on his money for a fixed interest rate and fixed term. This is commonly referred to as a "private lender" arrangement, which we'll cover in more depth in Chapter Six. Bob protects his interest with a lien on the property, and you are able to buy it and do what you wish with it. In this case, Bob may decide to fund 100% of the purchase price and repairs, or he might fund just part of it, while you use another source (hard money, a mortgage, line of credit, etc.) to cover the rest. Again, this depends on your strategy.

Let's look at a strategy that utilizes a "private lending partnership."

> The house was halfway across the country, but that didn't stop Kevin from moving forward on the four-bedroom home located 2,000 miles away. The only problem was this: Kevin had very little money with which to work and could not obtain a mortgage from the bank because he already had too many loans. The home was listed at just $45,000 and was already rented for $800 per month.
>
> Kevin had been building a relationship with a local retired real estate investor, Donald, for several months, so he decided to work out a deal. He and Donald agreed to a $45,000 loan at an interest rate of 8%, spread out over 30 years. The payment to Donald of $330 plus $120 for taxes and insurance brought Kevin's total monthly payment to $550. Setting aside $150 per month for vacancies, repairs, management, and capital expenditures, Kevin cleared roughly $100 per month in cash flow on this property with no money out of pocket.

4. Credit Partnership – In a credit partnership, Bob lends his ability to get a loan but doesn't supply any down payment. To accomplish this, you would use a hard money lender (see Chapter Five) or another private lender (see Chapter Six) to purchase a property, including repair costs. If the deal is good enough, this should be feasible; however, it is the most expensive option by far. After the home is rehabbed, rented, and producing good month-after-month cash flow, Bob refinances the home into a fixed-rate, long-term mortgage using his great credit, but both you and Bob remain on the legal title for the property.

Heather had never purchased a multifamily property before, but the duplex—listed at just $85,000 because of the bad smell inside—was too good to pass up. She knew it would rent for $1,000 per side after the $15,000 worth of necessary repairs were completed. However, without the ability to get a mortgage because of her bad credit, caused by a recent divorce, she felt stuck. Luckily, she didn't let the roadblock stop her. Heather contacted a local hard money lender (again, we'll talk more about hard money in Chapter Five) about the deal and explained her plan. At the same time, she mentioned the deal to her brother, Maurice, who didn't have a lot of money either but had excellent credit.

The hard money lender agreed to fund the entire $100,000 needed as long as the loan was for a maximum of one year. Heather brought just the closing costs ($3,000) to the table, and she and her brother bought the property and quickly fixed it up. After the property was rented out, they waited a required six months and approached a local bank. The bank agreed to finance up to 75% of the appraised value of the property, which came in at $140,000. This allowed Maurice—with his good credit—to obtain a loan for $105,000, enough to cover the hard money loan fees and closing costs.

Heather was able to put this deal together for no money out of her own pocket (or out of Maurice's) while gaining significant equity and great monthly cash flow, all because she didn't say, "I can't."

I have used all four of these Bob strategies to invest in real estate, and all four have worked out great. Yes, I am giving up part of my profit and cash flow to someone else. However, I believe 50% of a great deal is better than 100% of no deal.

Without Bob, I often find myself up a creek without a paddle. Bob gives me the security I need to sleep at night, keep moving forward, and do what I do best— put deals together. These partnerships also

50% of a great deal is better than 100% of no deal.

help teach other people how to "be cool" and gain a huge foothold in getting financially ahead. It's truly a win-win.

Before you invest in real estate through a partnership, you absolutely must speak with an attorney who specializes in this kind of thing, as well as a CPA who does the same. I'm not just saying this to protect myself as the author of this book—there are ways of structuring a partnership that can have *huge* implications on both your tax bill and your liability. Even something as simple as having your partner put in money at the wrong step can cost *you* thousands of dollars at tax time. So please, go speak with a knowledgeable CPA and lawyer. Doing so will cost a couple hundred bucks, but I promise it will be well worth it.

Dangers and Pitfalls of Using Partners

If you just finished reading about Bob and thought, "Perfect! This is so easy!" I've got some bad news for you: the theoretical is always easier than reality.

In this book, Bob is hypothetical. In real life, Bob is a real person, with his (or her) own goals, dreams, fears, agendas, time, creativity, and personality. As with any venture, once you insert the "human equation" into the picture, things can drastically change (for better or worse). Let's talk about some of the pitfalls of working with a partner to invest in real estate creatively.

1. **Personality Conflicts** – Partnerships can be difficult because of the possibility of vast differences in personalities. When

you are relying on another person to get things done, and you don't mesh perfectly, conflict can easily arise. For example, what if Bob ended up being controlling, irritating, and domineering? If you are investing in buy-and-hold real estate with Bob, you may need to spend the next 30 years tied to him and his personality problems. This is why picking the *right* partner is so important.

2. Differences of Opinion – Everyone has an opinion of how things should be done. If you are in a partnership, you are forced to compromise on many aspects of your business. From paint color to investment type, differing opinions can cause difficulty.

3. Suspicion/Trust – As in any close relationship, suspicion and trust issues can easily arise—especially when things aren't going well. Trust can be hard to gain and quick to lose. Fraud also plays a role in the demise of many businesses and partnerships. This is why keeping impeccable records is so important to any partnership. You may also want to plan on using a third-party bookkeeper to limit any suspicion of wrongdoing.

4. Delayed Decision Making – When you are acting alone, you have the ability to quickly make decisions based on how you want things. In a partnership, you are often forced to discuss every decision—no matter how trivial—with your partner, which can add a lot of time to your dealings. This is why I generally prefer Bob to be a "silent partner" and to understand from the beginning that I am the primary decision maker.

Of course, I want to discuss critical business issues with Bob, but I don't want Bob demanding that I talk with him before picking a tenant, paint color, or rental price. This conversation needs to happen very early in the partnership, before any money is spent, and must be written down and signed off on by both parties. I know my strengths, and I've been in the business long enough to generally know what I'm doing. That's not to say I don't value input, but I simply need the freedom to act quickly and decisively on non-major issues. If your partner cannot accept this, you may need to find a different partner.

5. Smaller Profits – When you form a partnership, your profits, by nature of the agreement, are split. In other words, you will make a lot less money per deal than if you were working alone. However, as I've said before and say often, 50% of a great deal is better than 100% of no deal.

The same is true for Bob. People may ask Bob why he would give me (or you) 50% of a deal when he could do it all himself, given that he is funding the total purchase. The simple truth is, Bob would not buy the property himself. Bob would continue going the way Bob has been going and would do nothing different—and Bob knows it. So for him, 50% of a deal I (or you) put together is better than 100% of sitting on the sidelines and buying nothing. Besides, Bob doesn't have to do much work for his part, and he gets front-row training from an experienced investor.

6. Mixing Business/Friendship – Often, people get into business with friends or family, and many times, that partnership becomes the death of that relationship. Partnerships don't always work out, and when they don't, the relationship is often destroyed for good. A partnership is very much like a marriage: don't get into it unless you're ready! Again, this is why setting your business up right from the start is so key.

As I mentioned earlier, don't be afraid to sit down with a lawyer for an hour or two to review your partnership agreement. Your partnership agreement is there to protect you from the things you don't think will happen, because something always will. When you have a plan for how to deal with problems, the risk of the relationship ending badly diminishes greatly, because both parties have already agreed on what to do.

For example, what if five years down the road, you and Bob jointly own a triplex, and you have a "hell month" when you have to evict one tenant, completely remodel her cockroach-infested unit, and remodel a second unit at the same time? This is exactly what happened to me recently. We had $10,000 saved up in an account for problems in business, and *poof!*, just like that, a "hell month" drained our account. An eviction, a paint job, and a trashed unit cleaned us out. However, because we had agreed ahead of time, and in writing, that we would split all such future losses (and that I would manage the situation), I simply talked with my partner, and we each wrote a check for half the overages. No one was upset; no one was confused.

If you don't prepare for issues like this, you might end up with some very awkward conversations, angry friends, and a sour business relationship.

7. **Unrealistic Expectations** – When you rely on someone else, setting expectations as to how something should be done is easy. However, when your partner doesn't live up to your expectations, it's easy to grow bitter and blame him or her. One thing I do to curtail this is to *consistently underpromise and overdeliver*. In fact, I generally don't promise anything at all. All I can do is show them what I've done in the past and give my best guess for what the future will look like. In reality, that's all real estate investing is: an educated guess. I will show them how I determined the potential cash flow or equity for a property, planning for the worst-case scenario, and make sure they understand I'm not promising that the deal will work out a certain way.

The only time this does not apply is in a pure lending partnership, when I am simply borrowing money at a fixed interest rate for a fixed term. In that case, I do promise to pay a certain rate for a certain time through a promissory note.

8. **Legal Responsibility for a Partner** – While the legal ramifications depend largely on the entity structure you establish and the choices you make at the beginning, you and your partner are still in business together, which means you are responsible for that person, at least as far as the business is concerned. If he or she skips town, you are still responsible for the whole business, and its obligations. Once again, this is another reason you must make sure your real estate attorney helps you draft any partnership agreements to help protect your interests and your financial future.

9. **More Complicated Taxes** – When you alone are running your business, the taxes and accounting requirements are much more simple than when you're working with partners. The more members you bring on as owners, however, the more complicated the bookwork becomes, and the more time consuming (and costly) tax season is. Consider this part of the "cost of doing business" and prepare for it. While you may have been accustomed to having your taxes done for $100 before, you should expect to spend $2,000 or more for this service once you start adding properties and partnerships.

Wrapping Up: Is a Partnership Right for You?

Partners are not for everyone, and not everyone will make a good partner. However, when you can use partners to move your business forward and close more deals, they are invaluable. Real estate investing is a relationship business, and without others, you will never succeed.

As I've demonstrated thus far, there are multiple ways to buy property using a partner with no or little money down. However, each technique involves its own trials and tribulations. Only you can decide for yourself the best way to put together each deal. No two deals are identical, so no two financing structures will likely be the same, either. Creative finance is a puzzle, and partners can be just the piece you need.

Finally, keep in mind that a great partnership cannot make a bad deal into a great one. You still need to find great deals and do your homework, ensuring a long-lasting and profitable relationship between you and Bob.

As we move on with more strategies for investing in real estate with no or little money down, I want you to always keep the partnership strategy in the back of your mind. Partners can play a role in any of these strategies outlined in this book, and a creative real estate investor's job is to find ways of putting together deals by mixing and matching strategies. The point of creative finance is to open your mind to new possibilities, and partners can open a whole new world of investing possibilities when combined with other methods. Let's move on to one of those strategies now: tapping into *home equity*.

CHAPTER FOUR: HOME EQUITY LOANS/ LINES OF CREDIT

If you already own your own home, and you owe significantly less than it's worth, you may have an incredibly cheap source of financing right at your fingertips. However, even if you don't own your own home yet, I encourage you to read this chapter in full because it will equip you with the tools you'll need to allow others to invest with you in the future.

Let's start at the beginning. What is "equity"?

Equity is the difference between what you owe on your property and what it could sell for. For example, if you owe $50,000 on your home and it is worth $150,000, you have approximately $100,000 in equity.

A home equity loan is a loan you can take out from a lender that is secured by the equity in your home. In other words, if you don't pay the loan back, the lender can take your personal home and resell it to pay the debt. A home equity loan is also known as a "second mortgage," because it is generally subservient to your primary mortgage. This means that in the case of a foreclosure, the primary mortgage would get paid off first, followed by the second. Before we get too deep into how to use a home equity loan, let's talk about the difference between the two types of equity products:

1. **Home Equity Loan** – A home equity loan is a mortgage product wherein all funds are disbursed at the beginning of the loan, with a definitive term length and equal monthly payments. For example, you may take out a $50,000 home equity loan at 3.75% payable for 15 years. The payment would be roughly $363 per month for the entire 15 years, or until you paid the loan off. You might think of a home equity loan as similar to a car loan or a normal home mortgage. These loans can have either a fixed (unchanging) interest rate or one that is variable (subject to change with the economy).

2. **Home Equity Line of Credit** – A home equity line of credit, or HELOC, is similar to a home equity loan, but even though you are allowed to borrow a predetermined amount of money, that money is not necessarily dispersed at the start of the loan. Instead, it is available for you to borrow and pay back with flexibility. If this is a bit confusing for you, don't worry. Let me give you a really simple analogy: think of it like a credit card. You can borrow money, up to a certain amount, and pay it back at will, though you are required to make at least a minimum payment each month based on the amount you have used. The minimum payment is often simply just the interest that accrued during that month, but some lines of credit require a higher payment than just the interest. For

example, you may have a $50,000 limit on your home equity line of credit, but you only use $20,000 of it. If your interest rate on the line of credit is 10%, your monthly interest payment would be $166.67 ($20,000 x 10% / 12). If you paid only the interest each month, your loan balance would never go down, because you would never be paying back the principal. A HELOC typically has a variable interest rate, though fixed rate versions are available.

Where Do I Get a Home Equity Loan?

Most banks and credit unions offer a loan or line of credit that can tap into your equity in your home, though these offerings may go by different names. Simply call up your local bank or credit union and ask to speak to someone in the lending department; then ask if they do second mortgages and what kinds they currently provide.

As of this writing, typical rates on a home equity loan hover around 6.5%, and adjustable rates on a line of credit hover around 4%. As you can see, a loan typically has a slightly higher rate, because you are paying for the security of never having your loan payment increase (as long as you get a fixed rate loan). Also keep in mind that not all home equity loans are "fixed," so be sure to ask your lender if the one you are considering is.

Equity: How Do I Find Out How Much I Have?

As the name would imply, a home equity loan or line of credit will require you to have equity to qualify. Therefore, let's take a few minutes to explore what equity is and why it matters. As mentioned earlier, equity is the difference between what you currently owe on your home and the fair market value of that home. For example, if you owe $50,000 on a home whose current value is $80,000, you have approximately $30,000 in equity (not including the costs required to sell the property if you wanted to).

In math terms, the equation would look like this:

Fair Market Value - Your Total Mortgage Balance(s) = Your Equity

When determining your ability to obtain a home equity line of credit, the most important number to clearly understand is known as "loan to value," or LTV. The LTV is a percentage that shows the ratio between what you owe and what the property is worth. The higher the percentage, the less equity you have. LTV is determined using the following formula:

LTV = Loan Amount / Fair Market Value

This calculation will give you a percentage, which is your LTV. So, revisiting the example I just used, if you owed $50,000 on a home worth $80,000, the calculations would look like

LTV = $50,000 / $80,000 = 62.5%

So, what is a good LTV and what is a bad LTV? In the crazy lending world of the mid-2000s, lenders were offering home equity loans and lines based on 125% of the value of a person's home, a 125% LTV. In other words, back then, if your home was worth $100,000, you could borrow as much as $125,000 in a home equity loan or line of credit. Lenders did this because they believed, foolishly, that prices would continue to rise and values would eventually increase enough to cover the loan.

I'm sure you can see the problem with this. In late 2007, the market began to change... fast. Home prices began to drop, and millions of borrowers who had borrowed far more than their houses were worth were suddenly underwater.[15] Even those who didn't

---

[15] Underwater: When the balance owed on a home mortgage is more than the home is worth,

borrow too much but obtained low or no down payment loans on their houses found themselves underwater. Consider also that many of these loans were adjustable rate mortgages and were offered to people who were not very good at handling their finances, and you can see why America nearly melted down.

Today, lenders have learned from the mistakes of the past, and the days of getting 125% LTV loans and lines of credit are gone. More typically, the highest you'll probably see is around 90% LTV, but even that may be difficult to find. In other words, if your home is currently worth $100,000, the bank will likely cap the total amount you can borrow across all loans at $90,000. So, if you have a first mortgage with a balance of $70,000, and the lender will allow you to borrow 90% (or $90,000 total), you could potentially obtain a loan or line of credit for a maximum of $20,000.

Keep in mind that as with nearly all loans, you will need to meet certain credit and income minimums to obtain the lending, and rates and terms will differ based on your LTV, debt, credit, income, and other factors. You may have a ton of equity in your property, but if you are rocking a 520 credit score, obtaining a home equity loan or line of credit will be nearly impossible.

Be sure to shop around to various banks when considering a home equity line of credit. In my small town, rates can vary by as much as 10% between banks. I feel sorry for all those people who are paying 13.5% at X Bank while I'm paying just 3.5% at Y Bank. Don't be like them. Get out there, make some phone calls, and shop around to get the best rate possible on your home equity loan or line of credit.

---

making it almost impossible to sell to a typical buyer without coming up with the difference out of pocket.

How to Use a Home Equity Loan or Line of Credit to Creatively Invest in Real Estate

I want to share some strategies for using your home's equity to invest in real estate creatively without needing to come up with much cash out of pocket. As with all the lessons in this book, this may or may not work for you, but understanding the concepts is key in becoming a proficient creative real estate investor.

The following are two of the most common techniques you could use if you have equity in your home. Rather than trying to explain what they are, I'll tell you two stories of investors who used their home equity to invest in real estate.

THE SUBSTITUTION: Shawn and Lynne were looking to buy a cash flow–friendly duplex that came on the market for $70,000. They also owned their primary residence free and clear, which means they owed nothing on their home (so their LTV was 0%).

Although they could have gone to a bank and taken out a loan on the investment property, they would have had to come up with approximately $21,000 out of pocket as a down payment (because their bank would lend them only 75% of the value, $49,000, the rest would need to be provided as a down payment).

Instead, because they owed nothing on their home, they talked to the bank and obtained a home equity loan tied to the value of their primary residence (*not* based on the new rental purchase) for $80,000, enough to pay for the cost of the entire purchase of the duplex and to cover the repairs the property needed.

They ended up with a fixed rate loan at 5.25% amortized over 15 years, for a monthly payment of $643. They are currently paying down the loan quickly, using the cash flow from the property, and plan to have the duplex paid off in less than seven years, with absolutely no money out of pocket.

In the story of Shawn and Lynne, they used the equity in their home to purchase a property "free and clear," meaning the investment property was paid for without a loan on that property (because the loan—the home equity loan—was on their primary residence, not the rental property).

Another neat strategy Shawn and Lynne could add to this would be to go to the bank after all the repairs have been completed and after the proper "seasoning" (the time a bank requires between refinances, typically 6-12 months) has passed and refinance the loan, putting the lien on the rental property and freeing up their personal residence home equity. For example, they purchased the home originally for $70,000 and used an $80,000 home equity loan (tied to their primary residence) to buy it. If they could get an appraisal to show a new value of $110,000, they could get their bank to refinance the property for 75% LTV and get a standalone mortgage on the rental property for $82,500. This would allow them to pay back their home equity loan—the one for $80,000 on their primary residence—and free up that equity to "rinse and repeat" the process, repeating the same strategy over and over as long as they could qualify for new loans, never using their own money. Obviously, this strategy is contingent on getting incredible deals for which you can "force" the appreciation higher through a rehab. If this is a strategy you plan to use, I would recommend using a home equity line of credit rather than a home equity loan, so you will be able to keep using the same line of credit over and over without having to get a new home equity loan each time.

Let's move on and talk about another strategy for using your home equity, because, frankly, most people looking to invest in real estate don't have as much equity in their homes as Shawn and Lynne did in the story I just told. In that case, is investing with a home equity loan or line still possible? Definitely. Let's look at another example of how an investor could use creativity and a *small* bit of home equity to invest without any cash of their own.

THE DOWN PAYMENT ASSISTANCE: Jessica was an experienced investor who owned a few properties but had most of her cash tied up in other ventures. However, when she received a lead for a killer deal, she knew she couldn't pass it up. Jessica would be able to buy a single-family home worth around $90,000 for just under $60,000. Unlike Shawn and Lynne and their free-and-clear home, Jessica already had a loan on her primary residence. She owned a home valued at $190,000 and held a mortgage for $125,000. Her local bank would lend up to 80% of the value of her home on a second mortgage, a home equity line of credit, meaning she could obtain a total of $152,000 in loans on her property. Because she owed $125,000, she was able to get a home equity loan for $27,000—definitely not enough to buy the rental property she wants, but enough to be creative with.

Jessica spoke with a different bank, and they offered her an investment property loan that required a down payment of 30% of the purchase price. This meant Jessica needed $18,000 down to buy the house. She didn't have that money in her checking account, but she *did* have it in equity in her home. So Jessica tapped into her home equity using the home equity line of credit she had taken out. Although she had approximately $27,000 in the line of credit, she used $18,000 of it to fund the down payment on the new investment property at 4% variable interest. Her new investment property loan was for $42,000 on a 5.25% APR, 30-year fixed mortgage (for a monthly payment of $231), while her line of credit required a monthly interest-only payment of $60, for a combined total monthly payment of about $291. The home now rents for $1,000 a month, providing significant cash flow, so Jessica can snowball the debt, paying off the line of credit first (because it's variable), followed by the loan on the investment property.

In this example, Jessica did not have enough equity to fund the whole deal, but she did have some. This allowed her to use several mortgage products to purchase the investment property.

If you ask most creative real estate investors, you'll find that one loan is seldom enough to get a deal done. Often, a creative combination of two or more different loans is needed to get a deal done, just as in Jessica's story. Yes, it is more complicated than a typical 20% down payment conventional loan that most people think of, but the end result can put you years ahead in the real estate investing game.

Let's move on and talk about a subject that many people have regarding home equity loans…

Can I Get a Loan or Line of Credit on an Investment Property's Equity?

The question is often asked: "Can I get a home equity loan or line of credit based on the equity in one of my rental properties?" After all, if you own a rental property worth $200,000 but only owe $100,000 on it, shouldn't tapping into this equity be easy?

These kinds of loans were common in the past, but today they are not as easy to find, though some portfolio lenders and hard money lenders may still allow you to obtain a second mortgage on a rental property. Just don't expect to walk into any bank and get one. It may take a lot of phone calls to find, if you even can.

Instead, many investors prefer a different strategy, wherein they use the combined equity from multiple properties they own to obtain a large business line of credit they can use for whatever business purposes they deem fit.

For example, let's say you own five rental properties, and each has a significant amount of equity:

	Amount Owed	Property Value	Total Equity
Property 1	$67,000	$89,000	$22,000
Property 2	$42,000	$97,000	$55,000
Property 3	$98,000	$155,000	$57,000
Property 4	$14,000	$80,000	$66,000
Property 5	$105,000	$200,000	$95,000
Totals:	$326,000	$621,000	**$295,000**

In this scenario, you would have a good chance of approaching a commercial bank or portfolio lender with a solid business plan and could potentially tap into the majority of this equity through a commercial or business equity loan or line of credit. To learn more about these kinds of loans, definitely call around and talk to various lenders, because each lender will have different requirements and programs that may or may not fit your business model.

Additionally, the rules for commercial and portfolio lending are very different, and much less strict, than for the residential world. Even if you don't plan on taking a loan out right away, it doesn't hurt to start the conversation with a lender today and begin building that relationship in preparation for your future needs.

Risks and Drawbacks of Using Home Equity

Life isn't all peaches and cream when you are dealing with home equity loans and lines. They sound great, but you need to understand the risks inherent in such loan products. If the funds are misused, tapping into your home equity can be disastrous to both your real estate investing business *and* your personal finances. Because a home equity loan is based on the equity in your primary residence, the lender can place a lien on *your home*; if you don't pay the money back, the lender will then foreclose on your home and kick you out on the street, severely damaging your credit in the process.

The obvious solution is to simply pay your bills. If you do, you don't need to worry, right? It's not quite that simple, actually. You need to be aware of a few more dangers and pitfalls. Don't let this information scare you, but you need to know about these risks so you can prevent yourself from making the same mistakes other investors have made.

1. Overleveraging

As you learned earlier, during the mid-2000s, banks were allowing homeowners to take out far too much equity in their home, a condition known as "overleveraging." Although banks are no longer providing 125% loans, many will still allow you to take out up to 90% of your home's value.

Is 90% too much?

That is a matter of personal opinion, but understand that values go up and values go down. As of the writing of this book, values are increasing around the country at a rapid pace. As a result, we may see a decline in values in the future (what goes up must come down!), though no future is certain.

If you obtain a 90% LTV loan on your primary residence and property prices drop 20%, you'll quickly find yourself underwater and will be unable to sell your home without coming to the closing table with a significant amount of cash or doing a short sale.[16]

Leverage can be a great thing, but overleveraging can be dangerous because it limits your options... The more options you have, the more opportunities you'll have for success.

Leverage can be a great thing, but overleveraging can be dangerous because it limits your options. If you don't plan on selling, and you have a fixed rate mortgage, being underwater may not be a big deal to you, because your payment won't change. However, overleveraging does remove options, and having options is key to success in real estate. The more options you have, the more opportunities you'll have for success.

2. Less Cash Flow

Additionally, by using your home's equity to fund a down payment or the entire purchase price of a property, you are decreasing the amount of cash flow you would normally receive. For example, when we talked about Jessica and her use of $18,000 of her home equity line of credit to fund her real estate down payment, note that her monthly interest-only payment on that $18,000 was $60 ($18,000 x 4% / 12 months). Although this is not a huge number, it is $60 less that Jessica gets to keep.

Therefore, if you plan on using your home equity to fund your real estate purchase (or even just the down payment), getting a killer deal on the property is even more imperative, to make up the

---

[16] Short Sale: A sale of real estate in which the lender agrees to accept less than what they are owed to allow the homeowner to sell. A short sale typically hurts the homeowner's credit.

difference.

3. Adjustable Rates

A third danger of home equity loans and lines is something I've touched on a few times already: the potential for an adjustable rate. Each lender will have different terms, rates, fees, and requirements for their loan products, but if you end up with a lender who offers only an adjustable rate loan, it's extremely important that you fully understand what you are getting into and the potential for what could happen. I call this Worst Case Scenario Analysis, and it's helpful to use when considering an adjustable rate loan. Essentially, I like to look at what the worst case payment would be for that loan, and if it would still make the deal work, I'll consider doing it.

Let's look again at the example of Jessica, who used an $18,000 home equity line of credit to fund her down payment. Because the loan was not fixed, her interest-only payment could change. If you were to look into the fine print of her line of credit (which Jessica did before taking out the line), you would discover that the line of credit was capped at increasing by no more than 2% per year, for a maximum interest rate of 24%. So, let's do a Worst Case Scenario Analysis on this deal and see how it pencils out:

- Current loan amount: $18,000
- Current interest: 4%
- Current minimum payment: $60
- Worst Case Scenario loan amount: still $18,000
- Worst Case Scenario interest: 24%
- Worst Case Scenario minimum payment: $360 per month

Wow! You can clearly see the danger of an adjustable rate loan or line of credit in this example. Jessica's initial payment was just $60, but if interest rates were to go crazy, she could end up paying closer to $360 per month for that money!

So the question is, is it worth it?

For Jessica, the answer was *yes*. She knew that the loan could only increase by 2% per year, so it would take a decade to reach its max, and as I mentioned earlier, Jessica planned on snowballing that debt and paying it off in just a few years. Additionally, Jessica bought a deal with an incredible amount of monthly cash flow, so she knew that even if the worst case scenario happened, she would still be able to make the payment using nothing but the cash flow.

The key to using the Worst Case Scenario Analysis is fully understanding the worst case scenario. Dig into the fine print from your potential lender and find out how bad things really could be. On a recent variable rate mortgage I received, I learned that the interest rate was capped at 11%, meaning it could never climb higher than 11%, no matter how high the market rates might rise. When I looked at the numbers and ran it through a Worst Case Scenario Analysis, I discovered that at worst, my payment would increase from $600 per month to $800, but because I'd be receiving almost $2,000 a month in rental revenue, I could handle the worst case scenario and receive slightly less cash flow if everything went sour.

Wrapping Up: Home Equity Loans and Lines of Credit

A primary home's equity can be a powerful tool for a real estate investor, but it isn't without some dangers to watch out for. The key to successfully using a home equity loan or line of credit is in comprehending exactly how it works, knowing the details of your particular loan/line product, and clearly understanding the risks of the particular loan product.

If you want to check out the latest home equity loans and lines, be sure to visit the <u>BiggerPockets Mortgage Center,</u>[17] which contains up-to-date rates for lenders across the country.

Home equity loans and lines can be great, but they depend on you (or a partner) having equity *and* the ability to get the loan. However, a traditional bank is not the only choice for obtaining a loan. In the next chapter, we'll look at a nontraditional method of financing that many real estate investors use and/or fear: *hard money*.

---

[17] http://www.biggerpockets.com/mortgage

CHAPTER FIVE: STRATEGIES FOR USING HARD MONEY

Imagine a world where you have all the funds you need, all the credit you could get, and banks pounding down your door to give you large sums of money for low interest.

That would be nice, wouldn't it?

The real world, however, is a much darker place. In reality, trying to get financing from a bank is often like trying to shave Chuck Norris's beard while he sleeps. It's just not going to happen (because he doesn't sleep). As they say, *necessity is the mother of invention*, and hard money is the invention birthed by the need for quick, uncomplicated financing. Although it is most popular among house flippers, hard money can also play an interesting role for any creative real estate investor willing to take the risk.

This chapter will explain what hard money is and how you can use hard money lending in your real estate investment business to do more deals and propel your business forward.

What Is Hard Money?

Hard money is financing that is obtained from private individuals or businesses for the purpose of real estate investments. While terms and styles change often, hard money has several defining characteristics:

- Based primarily on the strength of the deal
- Short term (typically 6–36 months)
- High interest (typically 8%–15%)
- Involves a high number of loan points[18]
- Often does not require income verification
- Often does not require credit references
- Much faster than traditional loans
- Property condition not important

If hard money is a new concept to you, you are probably reading the interest rates in that list thinking there must be some kind of typo. After all, compared to typical bank financing, hard money is *ridiculously* expensive! So why would anyone use it?

As I mentioned early on, necessity and simplicity. Hard money may be an expensive way to do business, but if those costs are factored into the final equation, it just might work for some people, especially given the simplicity with which an investor can obtain a hard money loan.

---

[18] Loan Points: Fees added by a lender to the cost of a loan that equal 1% of the loan amount per point. For example, if a lender required 2 points on a $80,000 loan, the fee would be $1,600 ($80,000 x .02).

How Do I Find a Hard Money Lender?

Hard money lenders generally exist in every market, but tracking them down can be a little tough. To help, BiggerPockets has created the Web's largest directory of hard money lenders, with lenders in all 50 states. To find this information, check out the BiggerPockets Hard Money Lenders Directory.[19]

You can also find hard money lenders by searching the Internet for "City Name Hard Money Lender." For example, a search of "Seattle Hard Money Lender" turns up numerous good results.

Another good source for finding hard money lenders is by speaking with other investors, agents, and mortgage brokers in your local market. Networking is a huge part of being a real estate investor, so don't be afraid to get out there and start building relationships and asking around for hard money referrals. You'll likely find that most real estate investors are eager to share their lenders with you, because this makes them look good in their lenders' eyes as well.

How Does Hard Money Work?

Often, house flippers will use hard money (as I have) to buy a property, fix it up, and resell it. When this approach works, it works well. The lender may charge 4 points (4% of the loan) and a 12% interest rate, but if that is figured into the total cost of the project, this number is just part of the price of doing business.

On the plus side, a borrower can obtain hard money in just a few days with minimal paperwork, no credit checks, and a lack of other formalities usually found in conventional lending. In other words, hard money *can* be very easy money, if your deal is strong.

---

[19] www.BiggerPockets.com/hardmoneylenders

Let me walk you through a typical scenario of how hard money works in the house flipping world.

Jane gets a really great deal on a three-bedroom home in rough condition, having her offer accepted at just $45,000. Her contractor gives her a bid of $35,000 to fully remodel the home, and Jane believes she can resell the house for around $130,000. However, Jane doesn't have the $80,000 needed to buy and renovate the home, and no bank will lend her the money on a home in such bad condition. Jane decides to pursue the deal using hard money.

Jane finds a local hard money lender who charges 4 points and 12% interest on a loan, for a maximum of one year. The hard money lender agrees to fund the full $80,000 for Jane, and the 4 points are added to the loan (remember, 1 point is equal to 1% of the loan; thus, $80,000 x .04 = $3,200), for a total loan amount of $83,200 and interest-only payments of $832 per month. Jane's contractor goes to work fixing up the property, and within six months, the home is sold for $130,000. Jane pays off the hard money loan and the closing costs, and she's left with roughly $30,000 in pretax profit on the flip.

(Keep in mind, this is not an in-depth discussion of the math regarding house flipping. For a much more thorough discussion on house flipping, don't miss *The Book on Flipping Houses: How to Buy, Rehab, and Resell Residential Properties*[20] by J Scott, published by BiggerPockets Publishing.)

---

[20] http://www.biggerpockets.com/flippingbook

This example is an ideal scenario when using a hard money lender for a flip, and many investors have similar stories. **However, obtaining 100% financing, as Jane did in our example, can be very difficult for a new investor**, though if the deal is strong enough, anything is possible. That's the beauty of hard money: there are few hard rules. We'll talk more about that in a moment, but first, this is all fine and dandy for house flippers, but what about individuals investing in rental properties? Let's explore how **buy-and-hold** investors can use hard money to invest in real estate with little or no money down.

Can a Buy-and-Hold Investor Use Hard Money?

No doubt you see the benefit of using hard money when flipping a house, but what about landlords and buy-and-hold investors? Should they ignore hard money?

By now, I'm sure you've caught on to a few major roadblocks for buy-and-hold investors in using hard money. The two biggest issues are

1. The short term
2. The high interest rate

After all, if you borrow $100,000 with a 15% interest-only payment from a hard money lender, you could be looking at a $1,250 monthly payment, compared with a 30-year bank loan at 5% for $536.82 per month—not to mention that the hard money loan probably needs to be paid back within a year or less. Talk about a cash flow killer!

Clearly, there are some issues to work through, but does this mean all is lost? Is hard money only for house flippers? No!

Buy-and-hold investors can definitely take advantage of certain strategies for using hard money in the right situations, which brings me to the story of my first flip, which accidentally taught me how to use hard money for a rental property. Let me explain...

Trouble on the Horizon

The house I found to flip was located on a nice street but had some serious problems, especially because the home had not been updated in nearly 50 years. Ugly wallpaper covered every surface, the floors were damaged and smelly floors, the roof leaked, the kitchen needed to be gutted, and the plumbing/electrical was a mess. This is not the kind of project I recommend for new investors. However, I was high off watching the flipping shows on TV and thought I could handle the project. Even worse, I decided I would quit my job to work on the property full-time.

Worst of all, I had one major problem: I was broke.

So I made some calls and discovered a hard money lender who would fund the entire purchase price and the total cost of repairs, so I could flip this house with nothing out of pocket. Although the money was expensive, I decided to do the deal anyway and jumped into the flip. Nine months later (ouch!), I wrapped up work on the project and listed the property for sale. (There are about a thousand other lessons to be learned here, but because this is a book about creative real estate investing, I won't go into them now. Just understand that this was a very "educational" flip!)

I now had a second problem: the market had changed. Prices were plummeting faster than I could drop my price, and I soon discovered I was going to have some major issues selling. The house sat on the market for months, and I finally realized I needed to do something. I didn't want to just sell it and make nothing, so I decided to get creative.

I decided I would become a buy-and-hold investor and rent the property out. I found tenants who loved the home and moved in. However, I still had the expensive hard money loan to deal with. I was in a tight spot, and I needed help, which brings me to the solution I've used a number of times since: I refinanced the hard money loan through a conventional bank. In other words, I was able to pay off the original hard money loan with a brand new long-term loan from a traditional lender.

I was able to obtain an 80% LTV mortgage on the property, which was enough to pay the hard money lender off in full. In the end, I ended up with a 4%, 30-year fixed loan, stable tenants, a beautiful house, and absolutely no money out of pocket. Furthermore, I now had time on my side; I could wait for the market to return rather than settle with making no profit.

Keep in mind that most banks will require at least six months (sometimes up to a year) of "seasoning" before they will allow a refinance to take place. In other words, even if you complete the repairs in two weeks, you will be stuck paying the high rates to the hard money lender for at least six months, but probably an entire year. Be sure to plan accordingly for this.

This might be a little confusing for you, so let me give you a quick, simple recap of what I did to make this strategy work. (Just keep in mind that this is only an *example* of something that worked for me – don't assume you can do this exact same thing. Remember – think of this as an art book, not a recipe book!)

- Found an incredible deal
- Used hard money to fund the purchase and repair costs
- Fixed up the home, adding more value than the repairs cost
- Refinanced the home, paying off the hard money loan
- Rented out the home for significant monthly cash flow

Will a Hard Money Lender Fund the Entire Purchase Price?

One question a lot of people ask is "Will a hard money lender really fund the entire purchase price *plus* repairs?"

Sure, it worked for me with my first almost flip—but will it work today, for you? That depends. Most hard money lenders want to see "skin in the game." In other words, they want to see that the borrower has some vested interest in the property's success. They want to know that the borrower has something of monetary value to lose. When you have nothing to lose, very little exists to keep you from walking away, and that scares hard money lenders.

However, 100% financing can still happen with the right deal. Remember, hard money lending has very few hard and fast rules, so everything is up for negotiation between the borrower and the lender.

> A hard money lender cares about one thing above all else: security. A hard money lender wants to know that no matter what, they are going to make money and win.

In the story of my first failed flip, I was able to secure 100% financing, including the repairs, because I had (what we thought was) an incredible deal. You see, a hard money lender cares about one thing above all else: security. A hard money lender wants to know that no matter what, they are going to make money and win. If I had sold the house, the lender would have received all their money back and had a successful investment. Had I defaulted on the loan, they would have been forced to foreclose and take the property for themselves, which they could then sell and make a profit. Again, another win for them.

So, the amount of cash you need to come up with to make the

"hard-money-to-refinance" strategy work depends largely on the deal you find. In general, most hard money lenders have a certain LTV they will lend on, which is usually between 50% and 70% of the after-repair value (ARV).

In other words, if the home, in good condition, would appraise for $100,000, the hard money lender would typically not lend more than $60,000 on the deal. So, if you found a property for $60,000, you might be able to get the entire purchase price covered, but you would have to come up with the closing costs and repair costs out of pocket. However, if you were to negotiate the same deal down from $60,000 and get the home under contract for $35,000, your chances are better that your lender will still fund $60,000, giving you the extra $25,000 for repairs needed.

Typically, this extra money would be given out in "draws" as the work was completed. So, you might replace the roof for $6,000, submit the receipt, and be reimbursed for the work (or the lender might pay the contractor directly, though this is uncommon). Again, this is designed so the lender has maximum security and feels they will win no matter what happens.

What If the Hard Money Lender Doesn't Fund the Whole Price?

If the lender will not fund the entire price, you have a few options:

- You can refuse to buy the property, forget this strategy, and move on.
- You can use your own saved cash to fund the rest.
- You can use money borrowed from another source, such as a partnership, equity line, credit cards, or other. Again, thinking creatively is important.

For example, if you can get a hard money lender to fund $50,000 of a $60,000 purchase, and you need an additional $10,000 for repairs, you are going to be short about $20,000. Could you borrow that money from a line of credit on your home? How about using a partner to fund that portion? What about partial seller financing (see Chapter Eight)?

As you can see, a *lot* of different options are available for using a hard money lender to get into buy-and-hold real estate with little or no money down. However, as I've mentioned several times, you need to be careful about some pretty important things when using this strategy. The next section will discuss four of them.

Risks and Drawbacks to Hard Money Lenders

Let's get this out of the way right now: hard money can be risky because of the high costs (both monthly and one-time fees) and short term lengths associated with the loan. However, understanding these risks is key to knowing how and when to use a hard money loan in your investment business. Let's look at the top four risks associated with using hard money...

You should view hard money only as a very short-term solution and factor the extra costs and monthly charges into the deal before making an offer on any property.

1. Hard Money Is Expensive – Although obtaining hard money is fairly simple if you find a great deal, the monthly payment can be prohibitively expensive. With rates ranging from 10% to 20%, your monthly payment will be double or triple what your normal monthly payment would be with a bank loan. This will almost guarantee a negative cash flow situation while you are holding the hard money loan.

This is why you should view hard money only as a very short-term solution and factor the extra costs and monthly charges into the deal before making an offer on any property. Let's say you borrowed a total of $100,000 from a hard money lender at 15% for 12 months using this strategy, and let's say the lender charged 5 points (5% of the loan amount) as an added fee.

$100,000 x .15 = $15,000 interest payments
+ $5,000 in loan fees (closing costs and points) =
$20,000 total cost of using the HML for one year.

Compare that to a conventional bank, borrowing $100,000 at 5% with only $3,000 in loan charges.

$100,000 x .05 = $5,000
+ $3,000 in loan fees (closing costs and points) =
$8,000 total cost of using a loan from a bank for year one

As you can see, using hard money in this case could cost you more than double what borrowing from a traditional bank would cost. Clearly, hard money is not a good option if you don't need it, but chances are, your bank financing will eventually dry up, and you may find hard money to be the best way to quickly close more deals with less money out of pocket, especially if you are a house flipper.

After all, if you can get $50,000 in equity on a property, is it worth paying $10,000 extra to do so? As with all creative methods of investing in real estate, you just need to get a significantly better deal on the property to compensate for the extra costs.

2. You Can't Sell – If you are using a hard money lender to flip a property, the most dangerous outcome is the inability to sell, which is exactly what happened in the story I told earlier about my first attempt at flipping. If you can't sell and can't refinance, you may have a significant problem on your hands. This is why clearly understanding your ARV is so important, so you know how much the home will sell for. Additionally, this is why speed is so crucial when flipping, because you don't want to give the market time to drop significantly (one of my many mistakes!). Finally, the easiest solution is to get such a great deal on the property that you can drop your price until it does sell and still make a profit.

3. You Can't Refinance for the Full Amount – If you are looking to use a hard money lender to buy a property, fix it up, and then refinance it into a rental property, the key is adding significantly more value than the cost of the repairs. For example, if you bought a home for $50,000 and put $20,000 into repairs, the home would need to appraise for *far more* than $70,000 for you to get your money back (because remember, banks only lend only a portion of the value, probably between 70% and 80% of the ARV). So, for you to fully pay off the hard money lender, the property you paid $50,000 for and put $20,000 into would probably need to appraise for at least $100,000 to get the full refinance.

What would happen if that home appraised for only $80,000 after the work was done? If the bank would lend 70% ARV, the most it would let you borrow would be $56,000, leaving you $14,000 short. You would then be required to pay that $14,000 out of pocket at the loan closing, or you wouldn't be able to refinance—and we aren't even talking about the closing costs you'd have to pay during a refinance.

This is probably the most significant danger in using the "hard-money-to-refinance" strategy, and again, it comes back to truly understanding your ARV. How confident are you that the $50,000 home you bought would actually appraise for $100,000 after you put $20,000 into it? Do you have multiple recent similar sold comps (similar homes that have sold; see Chapter Ten for a more in-depth look at comps and valuing property) to back that up? If not, don't even think about using this strategy.

4. You Can't Refinance at All – Another concern for those looking to use hard money to fund a future rental property is a complete inability to refinance at all. What if a bank turns you down for a loan because your debt is too high or your credit score is too low? Or what if the lending requirements change between the time you buy the property and the time you go to refinance it?

These are very real possibilities, so exploring all your options and having multiple exit strategies is important in case things don't work out. How little could you sell the property for and still get out okay? Could you add a partner onto the deal to refinance the property using that person's income/credit? For this reason, any time I use the "hard-money-to-refinance" strategy, I make sure the home could sell if I needed it to, and could sell fast. This means buying a home that people would want to buy and getting it for the right price. If no one in your area wants to buy two-bedroom homes, I would not recommend pursuing this strategy with a two-bedroom home.

Additionally, you will need to speak with a bank ahead of time and get preapproved for a loan, even though you'll be using hard money to buy the property. This means submitting all your paperwork to the bank and having it actually approve you for a loan. Things may change over the next six months, but this will give you a really good indication of your ability to get a loan.

Wrapping Up: Should You Use Hard Money?

Hopefully by now, you have a good grasp on the role hard money can play in your creative real estate investment strategy. As I've mentioned numerous times, the success of these strategies hinges on your finding an incredible deal. Incredible deals give you options— and options help you build wealth. If you do decide to pursue this

Incredible deals give you options— and options help you build wealth.

avenue, be sure you understand all the potential risks and that you adequately prepare for those dangers. Write your plan down carefully and be sure that everyone, including your hard money lender, is on the same page.

In the next chapter, we'll look at a close cousin to hard money— *private money*—and its potential role in funding your real estate deals with significantly fewer costs than hard money.

CHAPTER SIX: RAISING PRIVATE MONEY TO FUND YOUR DEALS

The "holy grail" of real estate finance, private money is not only an incredibly powerful way to scale a real estate business, but it is also a terrific way to do so without using any of your own cash.

However, raising private money is not easy, and you must follow numerous laws and complicated processes or you could risk spending time in the slammer (yes, jail!). Therefore, this chapter will give you a general overview of both how to raise private money and how to do so ethically and legally.

What Is Private Money?

Private money is money provided by nonprofessional lending individuals to fund your real estate deals. In other words, when "Rich Guy Gary" decides he wants to earn more interest on his cash than the 1% certificate of deposit his bank is offering, Rich Guy Gary may consider funding your next real estate investment.

This may sound similar to hard money lending (see Chapter Five) or partners (see Chapter Three), and the two categories do overlap significantly. In fact, the terms "hard money" and "private money" are often used interchangeably (many hard money lenders refer to themselves as private lenders or private money lenders). However, although the lines can be blurry, I believe there is a difference between private and hard money, and knowing that difference can save you thousands of dollars.

For the purpose of this book, I consider hard money lenders individuals who lend money as part of their business and charge higher rates and fees than a private lender might. For example, *hundreds* of hard money lending companies are listed in the BiggerPockets Hard Money Lenders Directory,[21] but *millions* of individuals in America have enough cash stashed away to fund your next deal. These potential private lenders generally keep their money in the stock market, bank accounts, IRAs, and other low-maintenance investments, because these individuals are not professional lenders, as hard money lenders tend to be.

Additionally, hard money lenders generally establish their official rates as a part of their business, whereas private lending leaves much more to negotiation and works to find a solution that fits both parties. Hard money lenders, as discussed in Chapter Five, generally charge 3–10 points (1 point equals a 1% fee) and 12%–15% interest, whereas most private lending is substantially cheaper and is often completely devoid of the points and fees.

The rate you pay your private lender and the length of your loan can depend on a number of factors but ultimately comes down to what the two of you agree to. Although no specific universal

---

[21] http://www.biggerpockets.com/hardmoneylenders

designations exist, the private money loans you will obtain typically involve three term ranges:

1. **Short Term:** Usually six months to two years; most commonly used for flips or refinances

2. **Medium Term:** Two to ten years; most commonly used for repositioning (improving, leasing, and refinancing) properties or other shorter projects when the lender doesn't want their cash tied up for too long

3. **Long Term:** More than ten years; most commonly used for buy-and-hold investments. Typically, these loans are the most difficult to obtain but can be the most beneficial for the buy-and-hold real estate investor. Rates are generally the lowest with long-term loans to make cash flow work on long-term investments.

Each lender has their own agenda and motivations, so you'll find that depending on the person you're dealing with, the term range preferred will vary. Let's talk a bit more about *who* private lenders are.

Who Are Private Lenders?

Most Americans know that there is tremendous power in real estate, and many would love to diversify into an investment that they feel is safe and secure. Even better, many Americans have a significant nest egg sitting in a 401k or IRA that could be used to invest in real estate.

Clearly, the money is out there. Therefore, your job as a private money raising investor is threefold:

1. Find those individuals.
2. Impress them with your personal brand.
3. Convince them of the strength of the deal.

Each of these tasks takes work and knowledge, so the rest of this chapter will focus on maximizing your skills in all three areas. Let's first focus on the task that many investors find the most difficult: finding private lenders.

How to Find Private Money Lenders

Private money lenders are all around. A recent study[22] showed that 22% of American workers have at least $100,000 in their retirement fund. With 154 million workers[23] in America, that means more than 30 million Americans have more than $100,000 in their retirement account, being shaken around by the stock market or accepting low fixed returns from CDs / annuities / savings accounts or other investments.

More than 30 million Americans have more than $100,000 in their retirement account.

We have numerous ways of finding these individuals, perhaps more ways than we can list here, but allow me to go through the four most common methods for finding individuals willing to lend their money for your next deal.

1. Family and Friends – Borrowing money from family members or friends is probably the most common way for new investors to get started with private money. However, this "low hanging fruit" carries with it some emotional attachments that can make success much more difficult to obtain if things are not done correctly. Only borrow money with those family members and friend who truly have money to lend. Real estate is risky, and I'd hate to see you lose Grandma Betty's life savings because a deal went sour. Also keep in mind the conversation we had back in Chapter Three about

---

[22] 2010 study by the Employee Benefit Research Institute and Matthew Greenwald & Associates, Inc.

[23] U.S. Department of Labor and Training

not asking for money. Especially with family, it's probably best to let them come to you. Many investors simply refuse to invest with family or friends, but the decision is ultimately yours.

2. Networking – As I mentioned earlier, 30 million Americans have $100,000 or more in their retirement account. These are everyday people you know: your doctor, dentist, school janitor, librarian, accountant, garbage man, and others. The key to finding private lenders in the general public is constant networking. Networking involves putting yourself out there, letting people know what you do, and talking about your business (and their life/business as well). If you don't already have a stack of business cards in your back pocket at all times, get some!

> *The key to finding private lenders in the general public is constant networking.*

Some of the best "official" places to network can be local real estate clubs, Chamber of Commerce meetings, BiggerPockets.com, and real estate–related conferences. However, your networking should not be limited only to official networking events; instead, networking should be a lifestyle. Let everyone know about your business and the great things already happening or that you plan to do. Carry pictures with you of recent renovations and purchases. Don't brag, but don't shy away from talking about your real estate successes (or goals, if you are just getting started) either.

Another great way to network is to provide valuable information for free. If you have a local real estate club, ask to speak and share what you know (but please, don't pitch! Simply provide value). If you don't have a local club, consider starting one. As I mentioned earlier, there is a lot of power in being a "connector" of people, so by starting a networking group where real estate professionals can meet one another and grow, you will gain a reputation as someone to be trusted.

3. Blogging – The same effort you put into networking in the real world can be applied online by teaching what you know. You don't need to be an expert to start a blog and share your story, but if you know how to communicate well online, a blog can be a great way to build up trust and gain a reputation. If the thought of starting a blog overwhelms you, understand that it can be done very simply, very quickly, and very cheaply.

While dozens of tutorials are available online that can teach you how to start a blog, I'd recommend starting by creating a BiggerPockets Member Blog,[24] which is hosted on BiggerPockets.com. You can be up and running in just seconds and can instantly have a targeted audience at your fingertips.

4. Public Record Search – Not everyone will be convinced that real estate is a good investment to have in their portfolio, but do you know who are the easiest folks to convince?

Yep, people who are already private lenders! A lot of people out there are already lending on real estate deals and may be willing to lend on yours, too. Although you can find these people through the methods already mentioned, you can also take a more direct approach and identify them through public records.

Each time a mortgage is made, the mortgage document is publicly recorded at the local county government. This information can be invaluable to you as an investor, because you can use it to find out who the lender is on any property. The majority of lenders will be listed with a bank name and address (Well Fargo, U.S. Bank, Bank of America, etc.), but others will be presented differently, with either a

---

[24] http://www.biggerpockets.com/blogs

person's name, an LLC name, or a trust. These are the individuals you are looking for.

In most counties, you can perform this search online through your local government's website, though this may involve a fee. If your county does not list this information online, you can simply go down to your county administrative offices and search manually (though this might take a lot longer).

Specifically, you are looking for the "grantee" (mortgage provider) line on the mortgage documents. You want to find grantee lines that have either a person's name or a corporate entity name (not the name of a bank). These are potential lenders. Doing a reverse address-phone search or sending a letter can put you in touch with these lenders and open the conversation, but use the contact information you find only to build a relationship. Soliciting others at random for money can be both illegal (for you) and annoying (for them).

How to Talk with Potential Lenders

Step One: Open your mouth.
Step Two: Start talking!

Seriously, don't overthink the idea of networking. When you are talking to people about your passion, let that passion shine through! Talk about why you love real estate, your goals, your dreams, but most of all, ask questions about the other person. Get them talking and sharing their goals. Listen for cues that they may be potential lenders for you.

Also, please don't start throwing the term "private lending" around to impress anyone. Raising private money is like dating—you don't want to ask the girl you've just met if she'd like to get married! Your goal is to build a relationship and see where that relationship leads.

When networking, remember this very basic idea: you are not a salesman asking for money. You are a business person holding an opportunity. Repeat this to yourself and seek to maintain this attitude when talking with people. You'll find that 90% of the people you chat with will not be good candidates for lending you money, and that's fine. You don't need to sell people on the idea; let the other 10% come to you because you have a good opportunity to earn really positive returns.

Raising private money is like dating—you don't want to ask the girl you've just met if she'd like to get married!

The Elevator Pitch

One of the most important techniques to use when talking with people is something anyone can and should adopt: the elevator pitch.

In conversations, one of the first questions to come up is "What do you do for a living?" This is the perfect opportunity to let the asker know and to open up the possibility of working together someday. A simple answer like "I run an investment company that focuses on purchasing, renovating, and renting out homes for monthly cash flow, and I work with a lot of different partners to make it all happen" can initiate a whole conversation on the topic if the person is interested. If not, no harm, no foul. If they want to know more, they'll ask.

In the business world, this quick synopsis is known as an "elevator pitch," and it is extremely important for a real estate investor to have one. An elevator pitch is a quick, less than 30-second explanation of what your company is and why it matters (it's called an "elevator pitch" because you should be able to deliver it completely in the short span of an elevator ride).

Remember, real estate investing is "cool" to a lot of people, and almost everyone is interested in earning more money. So let people come to you, and be prepared to answer any questions they may have. If they are extremely interested, they may ask you a lot of questions, which is great! This is all the more reason you need to take your real estate education seriously, because you never know when these conversations will occur.

Almost everyone is interested in earning more money. So let people come to you, and be prepared to answer any questions they may have.

When talking with people about your business, it's a good idea to say something like, "So, if you know anyone who's interested in lending on deals like this and working with me, definitely give them my number." This opens up the conversation so they can say, "You know, I might actually be interested in something like that" or "I know a guy who very well might be interested." Either way, the seed has been planted, and you didn't come across as begging for money—and you may just find some really valuable clients.

An important note: I don't recommend using these "elevator pitch" conversations to explain your whole private money lending process. As I said earlier, this is like dating. You probably don't jump into marriage right after asking a girl or guy out, and you probably shouldn't be making serious commitments at a networking event while you're surrounded by all the lights, sounds, and distractions. Use this opportunity to set up a time to get together, perhaps at your office or a local coffee shop.

Meeting with Your Potential Private Lender

At a more formal one-on-one meeting, you'll be able to much more easily explain the benefits and inner workings of your business. I recommend creating an information packet about what your company is and what you are offering. This is not a time to skimp on quality, so if your design skills aren't strong enough for you to create a nice-looking informational packet, hire someone to do it for you through a site such as eLance.com or oDesk.com.

Your informational packet should include the following:

- Your business name/contact information
- Your business mission/goals
- A description of how your business operates
- An explanation of how you use private money to fund deals
- Your track record, including photos
- Referrals from others you've worked with
- Expectations for both parties in the deal
- Anything else you can include to strengthen your position

Put all this information in a nice binder and simply walk through it with your potential lender. Let them know up front that lending relationships *are* relationships, and the point of your conversation is to see if you might be a good match, not to pitch something or pressure them into anything.

As much as this discussion is their opportunity to learn about your business, it is also a time for you to learn about their goals, expectations, and personality. Is the individual a nervous person who will be calling you every day for an update? Is the potential lender domineering and A-type, looking to push you around? Or will this person make a great lender with whom you can work multiple deals? Find out!

Your potential lender will also likely have numerous objections to lending you money, so you can either wait until these potential concerns come up or address them proactively. I'd recommend facing objections before they come up and including responses to them in your informational packet. After all, your potential lender may be thinking of those objections but never mention them to you—and will just simply disappear. By confronting those concerns up front, you can open up the conversation and enter more productive dialogues. Although the individual may have any number of concerns, the most common tend to be the following:

- What if the deal flops?
- What if the economy changes?
- What if you go bankrupt?

These are probably the most important questions you can answer for a potential lender. After all, they've heard the stories of real estate investments that crash and burn. No one wants to crash and burn. Therefore, you'll need to carefully explain the different ways and reasons their investment would be secure. For example, I might say the following to address most of these concerns:

"As you know, these are 'investments' that we're talking about, so there is no guarantee of success. There is risk involved with any kind of investment, but as our successful track record testifies, the way we invest in real estate seeks to minimize the risk at every turn.

"Most importantly, we offer a first lien[25] position on any property we lend on, which means if I end up being a thug and break any of the terms in our agreement, you could foreclose on me and take the property.

"Also, because of this lien, you will get all your money back, plus interest, before I ever see a dime. I only make money if you make money. Additionally, we will sign a promissory note that clearly and legally spells out all the terms and

---

[25] Property Lien: A legal notice connected to the recorded documents on a piece of real estate that lets the public know money is owed to the holder. All liens on properties must be paid off before a property can be sold.

conditions of our arrangement.

"Finally we only invest in amazing real estate deals that we will have significant equity in right off the bat, so we are protected against a drop in the economy. Because we buy only good deals, there is significant monthly cash flow following conservative estimates, and we set aside money each month for future expenses.

"All these factors help limit risk and ensure that your investment is as solid as possible."

By confronting potential objections up front, you are better able to help your prospective lender feel comfortable with you and your company.

I also think walking the potential lender through all the numbers on a particular deal is a wise move. Show them a printout of an analysis you've done, indicating the cash flow and return on investment you expect. Demonstrate that you've done your homework, and you will build the trust needed to make a great lending partnership. If you don't have a spreadsheet, I recommend trying out the BiggerPockets suite of analysis tools, which allow you to look at the potential profit, income, expenses, and other aspects of any real estate flip or rental property. These calculators also give you the ability to print out professional-looking reports to share with partners, lenders, and others. To learn more, visit http://www.BiggerPockets.com/calc.

Having a continuous pipeline of deals coming in is key, so your private lender doesn't have to wait too long for an opportunity.

Getting Your Private Lender to Commit

Once your lender has committed to the deal, it's time to get serious and make things happen. Many private lenders will feel passionate about the transaction right away, but if you let too much time pass, that passion will dissipate, and they may decide against investing with you, leaving you holding the bag on a property.

For this reason, having a continuous pipeline of deals coming in is key, so your private lender doesn't have to wait too long for an opportunity. Having the lender commit with their wallet as soon as possible is also wise. In other words, the sooner they have money invested in the deal, the less chance they will walk.

Several expenses occur on any real estate deal before the closing documents are signed (inspections, appraisals, insurance, etc.), so having the lender pay for these up front is a good way to lock them into a commitment, though this is optional.

Of course, you'll also want to get the agreement in writing, so plan on meeting with your private lender and an attorney at the beginning of your partnership.

How to Structure Your Private Loans: An Interview with Four Real Estate Investors

You can structure a private lending deal in numerous ways, far more than I could ever cover in this book, so rather than explain each one in theory, I want to introduce you to some other real-life investors who actually use private lending every day to run their real estate business. In this section, you'll meet four BiggerPockets members who have agreed to share how they've structured their private money relationships, so you can gain some insight into how you might structure yours.

However, before I get to their stories, let me make a quick disclaimer: you can structure a lending arrangement in many different ways, but legalities can differ by state and even by county. These four investors are all highly professional real estate investors, and all have sought legal counsel before devising their current system for raising money. It's vitally important for you to do the same—to sit down with an attorney to discuss your plans before you have an official meeting with your potential lender. Consider these interviews descriptive, not prescriptive.

1. Will Barnard – Barnard Enterprises, Inc.

 Will Barnard is a full-time, professional real estate investor and developer in Southern California. He currently specializes in flipping luxury homes with values above $1 million. Will has experience in almost every aspect of real estate investing, including spec building, rehabbing, wholesaling, landlording, short sales, land development, and notes. He conducts millions of dollars in real estate transactions each year, primarily using money raised from private lenders.

How do you use private money?

"Typically, I will locate a great potential real estate opportunity and present it to my private lenders, explaining the deal in detail. I don't utilize a "fund," but instead treat each deal separately and utilize certain lenders for each specific deal, sometimes using multiple lenders on one property by "fractionalizing" the note, which basically means the note is split between different lenders based on their contributions."

What kind of security do you offer your lenders?

"Each property we purchase is secured by a note and deed of trust, which gives the lenders the right to foreclose if I don't fulfill my end of the relationship. Typically, I never borrow more than 70%

of the total after-repair value, which gives the lenders a significant cushion against default. They are secured both by the deal and through the proper legal channels."

"Additionally, I always list each of my lenders on the property insurance as "additionally insured," so if something were to happen to the home and the insurance money was to cover the loss, I couldn't simply run off with the insurance settlement check."

What kind of legal entity do you use?

"My business is a legal corporation (Barnard Enterprises, Inc.), so the private lenders actually make the loan to my corporation."

Can you describe your money-raising process?

"Through consistent networking, I come across a lot of individuals looking for a secure place to diversify their portfolio. Whether it's online in the BiggerPockets Forums or in the real world at a local real estate club, people with money are everywhere. My goal is to simply offer advice and tell my story, and the money usually finds me."

"Once I have a deal under contract or am close to it, I send an email out to my private investor list, giving them the entire rundown of the deal, including the ARV, comps, repair list, repair costs, and the purchase price. I also provide the math for the LTV and how much of my cash will go into the deal. "

Most of my private investors started out as family, friends, and people I had a relationship with.

"I will also, on occasion, post a thread in the BiggerPockets Real Estate Marketplace[26] as well. Most of my private investors started out

---

[26] http://www.biggerpockets.com/marketplace

as family, friends, and people I had a relationship with. My web presence on BiggerPockets.com, my website, etc. also provided the opportunity to build new private investors."

"My goal when raising money is to attract repeat lenders. I want my lenders to be happy with every part of the deal so they'll come back to me time and time again."

What kind of terms and rates do you offer?

"Typically, the terms are 6–12 months and 10%–12% annual interest, with interest and principal due in one balloon installment on maturity date."

What kind of problems have you run into, and how have you overcome them?

"I have done a few loans over the past year that had interest-only payments rather than balloon payments. Due to longer holding times and holding costs, this has created cash flow and operating capital depletion at times."

"I have had to borrow more money to complete rehabs to resolve this issue and, in the future, will likely not do any loans with payments. Other than that, I have had little to no problems, and all investors have been paid back both principal and interest every time."

Learn more about Will Barnard and his luxury house flipping model by listening to his full interview on the BiggerPockets podcast at BiggerPockets.com/show32. You can also connect with Will through his BiggerPockets Profile[27] or through his website at BarnardEnterprises.com

---

[27] http://www.biggerpockets.com/users/BarnardINC

2. Brian Burke – Praxis Capital, LLC

 Brian Burke is co-founder and managing director of Praxis Capital, LLC, a real estate private equity investment firm created to provide high rates of return to his investors while tactically managing risk. He has been a real estate entrepreneur since 1989, purchasing more than 500 properties valued at over $150 million, primarily from foreclosures.

How do you use private money?

"I use private money in three different ways: I borrow it in the form of a private money loan (Loan); Blind Pool Funds (Blind Pool); and in identified asset funds (One Off). Both Blind Pools and One Off deals are considered a "fund," but in the case of a Blind Pool, the money goes into a pot, and I buy whatever I want with it, so long as the parameters of the deal match the fund objective. In the case of a One Off, the asset is identified ahead of time, and the fund is assembled for the sole purpose of acquiring that asset and executing the predefined strategy."

"On a Loan, we use one investor per loan per property. In the case of a fund, it could be funded by one person, but more often than not, it is funded by multiple investors into a pool."

What kind of security do you offer your lenders?

"In the case of Loans, the source of funds is truly a lender, and the security they receive is a first deed of trust on a single property. I use this strategy to leverage the equity in my Blind Pool funds with debt. In this case, the fund buys a property for cash, then borrows money from a private lender who gets a first deed of trust, and the cash goes back to the pool to purchase more assets. In the case of the

Blind Pool and One Off, those investors are not lenders, they are limited partners, and they receive no security other than an ownership interest in the entity."

"The entity will own all of the acquired assets, so there is real estate behind their investment, but no direct security, as there is in the case of a Loan. Hence, the Loans are not securities, and the investments into the funds are."

What kind of legal entity do you use?

"For a Loan, my ownership entity, either a Limited Partnership (LP) or Limited Liability Company (LLC), is the borrower, but no entity is formed for the purpose of the loan. The lender is either an individual, trust, LLC, corp, or whatever the lender uses (that's up to them, and it doesn't matter to me)."

"In the case of the Blind Pool, I typically use an LP, but that is only because I'm in California, and the LLC fees are high for entities that make a lot of income. Outside of California, I use an LLC. My management entity is the general partner of the LP (or managing member, in the case of LLC), and the investors are limited partners or LLC members."

Can you describe your money-raising process?

"In the case of a Loan, they write a check or wire money to the title company, and when escrow closes, we receive the funds. In the case of a Blind Pool or One Off, the investor writes the check or wires the money to the LP or LLC, and the money goes in the account."

"We have control of the funds and use it to make purchases (Blind Pool) or close on the transaction (One Off)."

What kind of terms and rates do you offer?

"Loans are 8% with interest-only monthly payments, and the principal is due in one year. Funds vary by the deal. Terms range from 30% to 70% splits of the profits; some funds offer an 8% preferred return, some do not."

What kind of problems have you run into, and how have you overcome them?

"The biggest problem is recruiting new investors. I have a full-time employee as my director of investor relations, and his job is to conduct outreach to current and future investors."

"Deal structure is the one thing that most new investors seem to get hung up on, but deal structure is simple compared to recruitment. That said, they are directly related to one another. If your deal terms don't match the appetite of your audience, the project won't get off the ground."

"I have one fund that offers investors 30% of the profits, and initially, there was a lot of resistance on behalf of the potential investors, because they thought they weren't getting a big enough share. I combated that in two ways: first was to offer funds with different strategies that had richer profit splits (70% to the LP), and the second way was to show that despite the fact that one fund had a 30% split, the investors are earning over 20% return consistently."

It's about having a menu of options for investors so that they can choose the right fit for their situation.

"Some investors don't care about the return, they just want a larger split, so we have something for them. Some don't care about the split, they just want high returns. We have something for them, too. Some investors don't want to tie their money up for longer than a year. We have a product that meets that criteria. It's about having a menu of options for investors so that they can choose the right fit for their situation."

To learn more about Brian Burke, listen to our full interview with him on the BiggerPockets podcast at BiggerPockets.com/show3. You can also connect with Brian through his BiggerPockets profile[28] or on his website at Praxcap.com.

3. Glenn Schworm and Amber Higgins – Signature Home Buyers, Inc.

 Glenn Schworm and Amber Higgins, a husband and wife team, are the owners of Signature Home Buyers, Inc., a real estate investing company based in upstate New York. Glenn and Amber's business focuses heavily on flipping houses. Over the past several years, they have successfully flipped more than 100 deals using private money.

How do you use private money?

"We have raised over $2 million in private lending from average people, not lending institutions or savvy investors. We use the financing to fund our real estate flips. We finance 100% of the deal, including purchase, renovations, and some holding costs with the cash we raise."

What kind of security do you offer your lenders?

---

[28] http://www.biggerpockets.com/users/cirrusav8or

"The lenders receive a note and mortgage for security on the loan. We also give the investors an insurance certificate made out to them so they know they are also protected with insurance in case of a total loss."

What kind of legal entity do you use?

"We are a subchapter S corp. It is how we started and still operate to this day."

Can you describe your money-raising process?

"When someone shows interest in investing, we mail them a professional packet explaining who we are and what we do. If they are local, we suggest they come and spend a little time with us, touring some of our current projects. At the end of that tour, we ask them, 'Are you ready to invest with us?'"

"We typically take a minimum of $100,000 or more to start. If they have concerns, we suggest they start with one house and see how it goes for them. We tell them if they like the process, then they can do it again and again, as long as they would like. If they are ready, we put them in our queue, and when the next house comes up that is close to the money they can invest, we let them know we are almost ready."

"When we have a close date in place, we ask them to wire the money to our attorney's office to be held in escrow until the closing. At closing, our attorney uses the funds to make the purchase, then they wire us the difference with our closing statement. Remember, we borrow enough for the entire project up front. Then the investor gets their note and mortgage for their protection."

"Each month, we send them a statement to show what their

investment is accruing. At the end of the term, when we sell the house and close, we wire the principal and interest back to the investor, and we look for the next deal."

"When we began, we did not have multiple investors on a project. However, once investors begin to grow their portfolio, we usually need to break it up on multiple houses in order to keep them fully invested. We try to not have more than three on any one deal. They are all individual mortgages, all in different positions."

What kind of terms and rates do you offer?

"We pay from 8% to 14% annually. However, we only pay for the months we use it. It is a fixed rate, so the investors get paid whether we make money or not. When we were new, we paid higher rates, as we were a riskier investment, but now that we have a long, solid track record, we can pay less, as we are a much more secure investment."

"All investors are paid at the end of the term in full. Our mortgage with investors is set up for a maximum of one year; rarely have we gone over, but when we do, we make sure the investor knows our plan, and their interest gets compounded starting on day one of the second year. We ask for an extension if necessary."

What kind of problems have you run into, and how have you overcome them?

"The only problem I can think of is selling a house for less than expected, or holding it much longer than anticipated and having to bring money to the table in order to pay the investor. It is not fun, but it has happened."

"My advice to all investors who use private investors is simple. *Always* pay your investors, no matter how good or bad you do on the deal. They have a set rate, and that is their investment. You have the risk of making it profitable, and if you do your homework up front and run the job efficiently, you should make more than the investors to make it a win-win."

"However, if everything goes wrong, never screw your investors out of their money, or you will soon be out of business, and you will give us all a black eye! Treat your investors like gold, because they are the lifeblood to your business. Always send gifts at Christmas and birthdays. Make them feel special. Do what you say you will do, and you will build a huge base of investor money to grow your business as large as you want it."

Always pay your investors, no matter how good or bad you do on the deal.

To learn more about Glenn and Amber, be sure to listen to our full interview with him and his wife Amber on the BiggerPockets podcast at BiggerPockets.com/show15. You can connect with Glenn on his BiggerPockets profile[29] or on his website at SignatureHomeBuyers.com.

4. Dave Van Horn – PPR The Note Co.

Dave Van Horn is the president of PPR The Note Co., an operating entity that manages several funds that buy/sell/hold residential mortgages, both performing and delinquent. Dave has been in the real estate business for 25 years, starting out as a realtor and contractor and moving on to everything from fix and flips to raising private money. Dave currently raises millions of dollars from private investors in the rather unique niche of real estate note investing.

---

[29] http://www.biggerpockets.com/users/glennschworm/

How do you use private money?

"I started by raising money from one investor for one property. Then I started doing private placements for real estate deals, and then I started doing them for notes. So for me, it was a natural progression. Although I started by doing one-offs, today, as a company, we use private money in our fund."

"I suggest hosting Investor Open Houses (Q&As) to provide investors with the opportunity to "see under the hood" of the business. We like to encourage transparency, and hosting these events is something that our investors have really shown an appreciation for."

"We attend a lot of events and strive to teach people about raising money, for example, self-directed IRA events. Teaching people your business model and how you raise capital is actually a great way to raise money. Raising capital for charity is another great way to mingle with the accredited. Another great way is to join CEO and networking groups."

Do the right thing, do what you say, and spend the money to hire a securities or real estate attorney to get the paperwork done right.

"Developing a solid reputation is very important. With other people's money comes more responsibility, especially since it is their hard-earned money or retirement money. Even if you are a private offering, and reports aren't necessary, constant communication with investors (before, during, and after) is still the way to go, and it also keeps retention up."

"Do the right thing, do what you say, and spend the money to hire a securities or real estate attorney to get the paperwork done right. I do the same paperwork regardless of who's lending to whom."

"If I'm lending money, I use the same paperwork that I require of my lenders."

What kind of security do you offer your lenders?

"A property or a note is collateralized through the recording process at the underlying asset's county courthouse. Equity investors in our fund are collateralized by a blue sky filing in the state that they're from. In other words, our investor's capital is collateralized by the assets of the LLC that's tied to the offering (i.e., they own shares of the company)."

What kind of legal entity do you use?

"We use an LLC structure as part of our private offering. The owners are Class A members who own more than 50%. All other classes of members are equity investors. We use a securities attorney to set up the private placement and register all the filings, including our blue sky filings."

Can you describe your money-raising process?

"If we're tying a lender to a property or an individual note, funding is wired at the time of closing, when it's going to be recorded."

"For an interested investor of our note fund, the process usually starts with an interview with our Investor Relations Department to see if there's a qualified fit. If so, we provide this accredited individual with a link and secure access to our private placement documents, which includes the offering, operating agreement of the company, purchaser's questionnaire of eligibility, W9, ACH form, signature pages, etc. The offering includes risk disclosures, our business plan, and a descriptive use of proceeds. The offering explains how everything works…the fund, the company, etc. If they want to move forward, they fill this paperwork out and send it in (via mail, email, or fax)."

"They submit their subscription agreement and fund their involvement with certified check or wire. We pay our investors a flat return every month, whether the money is in use or not. We utilize capital from the fund to pursue deals as they come up."

What kind of terms and rates do you offer?

"In our note fund, our current offering is for $15 million. It's a three-year term with a set preferred return of 11%, which is paid monthly via ACH. The minimum investment is $10K, $5K a share."

"When we borrow against an individual note or lend on a property, our rates and terms vary."

What kind of problems have you run into, and how have you overcome them?

"We once had an unforeseen expense, when we had to hire our securities attorney to review the investor content on our website in reference to our fund. To avoid this, be careful with the content you make available online for investors, especially if you have a private offering."

No matter how you plan to raise money, it's essential that you have your paperwork in order to avoid legal problems.

"We've learned from other decisions we've made along the way as well. For example, we used to have higher minimums, but we learned that people usually prefer to have their money spread out, so we actually received more investor capital after lowering our minimums. We also tried to pay investors quarterly until we found out that they actually prefer a monthly payment."

"Also, we used to have multiple rates and categories in each offering, but today, we keep it simple."

Learn more about Dave Van Horn by listening to the 28th episode of the BiggerPockets podcast at BiggerPockets.com/show28 and by checking out Dave's BiggerPockets profile[30] or visiting his website at www.PPRNoteCo.com

Legal Issues with Raising Money

Alright, it's time to talk about the legalities of raising private money. This is a highly regulated industry, and I am not a lawyer, so I strongly encourage you to speak with one before attempting to raise money.

The biggest legal issue you may encounter is that of "soliciting for money" (publicly asking for money). Over the past 80 years, some extremely strict laws have been passed that govern the advertising of money in the United States, but the laws are changing, and the legality of "general solicitation" is transforming almost daily because of the JOBS Act. However, even with the JOBS Act, you still need to follow numerous rules and conditions before you can advertise for money (such as only allowing verified accredited investors[31] to invest).

If you are just starting out, you would be best off steering clear of

---

[30] http://www.biggerpockets.com/users/davevanhorn/

[31] Accredited Investor: Someone who has $1 million in net worth or makes $200,000 per year ($300,000 for a married couple).

the "general solicitation" game and just saying no to publicly advertising that you are raising money. Once you get more experienced, you can jump into that game. Instead, raise money by allowing people to come to you, as we've discussed. If you network and let people know what you do, they will come to you if they want to invest. We've already covered this extensively: it's all about building relationships.

No matter how you plan to raise money, to avoid legal problems, it's essential that you have your paperwork in order. Sit down with a qualified attorney to discuss the correct legal entity, paperwork, and what you can and cannot do when raising funds.

Examples of Using Private Money for Investing in Real Estate

I love to step outside the theoretical and get down to the real world, so in this section, I will outline three scenarios of how private money can be used to fund your real estate investing business.

> **SHORT TERM:** Ivan is a house flipper in Southern California, where the typical run-down house costs over $300,000, which Ivan doesn't have. Instead, Ivan networks at various SoCal real estate events and meets individuals looking to invest in real estate without getting their hands dirty.
>
> On his newest flip, he talks with Dr. Jim, an anesthesiologist, who has over a million dollars in various investments and retirement accounts. Dr. Jim has no time to invest but is looking to diversify his portfolio. He lends Ivan $370,000, enough to purchase Ivan's newest flip and fund 100% of the repairs. Dr. Jim obtains a first lien position on the home, and Ivan signs a two-year promissory note, paying Dr. Jim 9% and payments deferred (but interest accruing) until the home is sold.

The funds are disbursed, and Ivan gets to work managing the flip. Within nine months, the property is rehabbed and sold, and Dr. Jim receives his money back, Ivan makes his profit, and everyone is happy and ready for the next deal.

In this example, Ivan uses a short-term private money loan to fund a real estate fix and flip. This is one of the easiest-to-obtain private loan to obtain because it gives the investor their money back in the shortest time possible. Ivan was able to avoid paying extremely high rates and fees from a hard money lender and could make more cash when the rehabbed property was sold.

While the flip in Ivan's example took just nine months from beginning to end, sometimes loans that short just don't work for certain strategies. Let's look at another example, this one of an investor who uses private money to invest in rental property.

MEDIUM TERM: Sarah is an investor in the Dallas area who is primarily interested in small multifamily properties. She is especially interested in finding properties that have been poorly run and poorly maintained, acquiring them for a low price, rehabbing them, and renting them out while she waits for the market to improve. Sarah finds the perfect property, located near her home—a garden-style fourplex in a great neighborhood that needs some new paint, carpet, and better management. She gets the property under contract for $110,000 and sets out to find funding.

She discusses the deal with an experienced investor, Wilson, whom she met online through BiggerPockets.com. Wilson is tired of dealing with tenants and has been selling off his properties. As a result, has a sizable chunk of cash in his bank account that he needs to "put to work." Wilson lends Sarah $130,000, enough for

Sarah to buy and rehab the fourplex, for a five-year term at 8%, interest only, which comes out to $866.66 per month.

Sarah immediately improves the property and rents out each unit for $750. After all the expenses, including the loan payment to Wilson, she clears almost $700 per month in cash flow. She then holds on to the property for several years, until the market improves, and then sells the property for $190,000, clearing a huge profit.

In this story, Sarah uses private money for a five-year term, which gives her time to get in and fix the property up, rent it out, and wait for the market to improve.

Let's look at one final example, which involves a much longer term. This is perhaps the most difficult type of private lending to obtain, but it can be golden to your investment strategy if you find it.

LONG TERM: Real estate investor Robert enjoys renting out single-family homes but has long since maxed out his "four property" limit from the banks. Instead, he uses private lending to buy cash flow–generating properties. He gets his newest project—an older, rent-ready, three-bedroom, two-bath home outside of Milwaukee—under contract for $50,000.

He then talks with his newest private lender, a distant cousin named Cal, about the property. The cousin made a killing selling his tech business in the late 1990s and has been investing his money in the stock market ever since, averaging a 6% return over the past decade. In an effort to diversify his portfolio, Cal mentioned at a recent family reunion that he'd love to get in on the real estate action. Robert and Cal agree to a 30-year fixed loan at 6%, but to sweeten the deal, Robert offers Cal 20% of whatever profit is made at the end. They close on the property, Cal makes his 6%, while Robert rents the home out for $1,000 per month and sits back to wait for his wealth to build. Fifteen years later, Robert sells the home for an $80,000 profit, and Cal receives $16,000 of that profit.

As you can see, these three examples were very different, but they all had one thing in common: a great deal. As I've said time and time again in this book, a great deal is the best foundation for creative investing. Because all three of the examples involved solid deals, the lending arrangement was a win-win for all parties, and the relationship could continue for many more deals.

Risks and Drawbacks to Using Private Money

Although using private money is a smart way to invest in real estate without using your own cash, it's not a perfect solution. This section will explore some of the risks of using private money, so you'll get the full picture and decide if this is an avenue you want to pursue.

Borrowing from real people always involves the potential for drama, emotion, and problems.

Legality – The legality of raising money is not easy to understand, and it differs largely depending on your location. Because of this, we advise using a lawyer, and as we all know, lawyers are not cheap. However, hiring a lawyer to set up your business correctly at the start is much better than not doing a deal at all or sitting in a federal jail cell for doing it incorrectly.

Networking Required – Networking is neither easy nor quick.

As I have noted, networking is a lifestyle, and if you don't like that lifestyle, you may find the process of raising private money cumbersome and difficult.

Higher Interest Rates – Although the rates you and your private lender agree on may not be as high as those you'd pay with a hard money lender, chances are the rates will be significantly higher than you'd see with a conventional bank. Typical private money interest rates I see are between 6% and 12%, depending on term length and other circumstances. If these rates fit your business model, great!

Personalities Are Involved – When borrowing from a bank, you are typically dealing with a system that has no emotion involved. However, borrowing from real people always involves the potential for drama, emotion, and problems. What if your lender suddenly needs his money back? What if they get into legal trouble? These scenarios are further evidence that you need strong written legal paperwork with any lending arrangement.

Should You Use Private Money?

Private money is not for everyone, but if it's an avenue you want to pursue, it can be a terrific way to raise enough capital to really scale your business to new heights. Be sure you understand the risks involved and take the necessary steps up front (ahem, *lawyer*) so you don't get into trouble at the end.

Finally, just remember that raising private money is about having great deals, building relationships, and ultimately delivering on the promises you've made. If you can do those three things, you'll have a successful future as a private money–funded real estate investor.

Next, let's move on to a strategy that involves investing in real estate without actually ever owning any property: *lease options*.

CHAPTER SEVEN: LEASE OPTIONS

The purpose of this book thus far has been to show you ways of buying real estate without using much (or any) of your own money. However, you can also invest in real estate without actually owning any property, using a technique known as a *lease option*.

This section will provide an overview of what a lease option is and how it works, and then we'll focus on how you, the creative investor, can use the lease option strategy to invest in properties that have significant cash flow potential with no (or low) money down. Keep in mind that a real estate investor could be on either side of the lease option arrangement, so getting a well-rounded education on what a lease option is from both sides is best.

Let's get started.

What Is a Lease Option?

A lease option involves leasing a home to someone with a legal agreement that stipulates that that person has the exclusive right to buy the home within a certain time period. The homeowner cannot legally sell the property to anyone else during the period defined by the lease option.

You may have also heard the term "rent to own" which is the more casual phrase used to refer to a lease option. I generally avoid using the term "rent to own" when talking with investors (I don't want to get it confused with the rent-to-own furniture stores!) but when talking with potential renters, I will use the phrase "rent to own" because it's more well known than "lease option."

Similar to a lease option, a "lease purchase" is a more formalized agreement wherein the property owner and the tenant sign a legal purchase agreement with a far-off closing date. Therefore, a *lease option* gives the lessee the choice of buying the property if they so choose, but they don't have to, whereas a *lease purchase* legally binds both the buyer (the lessee) and the seller to fulfill the terms of the contract. For the purpose of this chapter, I'll focus primarily on the *lease option*, because it is far more widely used, though keep in mind that both possibilities do exist.

For years, investors have used lease options to sell property to tenants who could not quite qualify for a loan. This process allows the tenants time to save up the required down payment, build their credit, establish a longer job history, or repair whatever is prohibiting them from obtaining a mortgage. A lease option could allow a family to move into their dream house and give them time to save enough for a down payment to buy the home, without worrying that the homeowner will sell to someone else in the meantime.

In case you are confused, let me give you an example of how investors have traditionally used the lease option:

John and Sally are a hardworking young couple who desperately want to buy a home, but they don't yet have enough money saved for the full down payment they would need. Additionally, John only recently started a new job, and the bank won't give them a loan until he has been there for one full year.

So John and Sally decide to do a lease option on a nice house in the suburbs. Jacob, a real estate investor, offers the couple a lease for $1,400 per month with the option to purchase the home anytime in the next three years for $140,000. During this time, Jacob cannot sell to anyone else, and as soon as John and Sally are ready and able, they will obtain a mortgage and purchase the home for $140,000, using a loan from the bank. Jacob will get his cash; John and Sally will get their home.

The Two Sides of a Lease Option

As you can see from the example of John and Sally, a successful lease option arrangement can be a win-win for all parties involved, but setting up the lease option correctly from the start is imperative to a successful operation.

The term "lease option" can be a little confusing, because it's not actually just one concept—it combines two independent real estate transactions:

1. A lease

2. An option

Although creating a lease option agreement using one document is possible, most investors choose to use two completely separate documents to create the agreement.

The lease portion is similar to any other lease that a landlord and a tenant might sign. The lease document would contain information such as the names of both parties, the property address, the monthly rental amount, rules and regulations, late fee information, due date, and more.

The option portion, however, involves a separate legal document in which the owner agrees to give the lessee the exclusive right to purchase the property within a specific time period and for a predetermined price.

Remember, however, that this option contract only gives the lessee the *option* to buy the property—it does not legally require them to. However, the option *does* legally obligate the seller to sell the property under the terms set forth in the option if the lessee does decide to move forward and purchase the property. In other words, the option is only "binding" for the owner.

In addition to the option paperwork, there is an option fee. When a lessee signs the lease and option agreements, typically, they will also be required to pay the rent, the security deposit, *and* the option fee. This fee is an up-front charge, similar to a down payment, found in most lease option arrangements. By paying this fee, the lessee is essentially paying for the right of exclusivity on the home, so only they can buy the home, and the seller cannot sell to anyone else.

The option fee amount can be whatever the two parties agreed on, but typically, the fee ranges from $2,000 to $5,000, depending on the value of the home. When you are the lessee in such an arrangement, negotiating the lowest fee possible, maybe even $1, is obviously in your best interest.

This fee is generally nonrefundable but will be later applied toward the lessee's down payment when the time comes for them to get their mortgage. If the lessee never obtains a mortgage and decides not to carry out the purchase option, the homeowner keeps the fee.

Why Lease Options?

We haven't yet discussed the best way for investors to use a lease option to invest with little to no money out of pocket, but don't worry, I will get into that soon. I want to be absolutely sure you fully understand how a lease option works before we talk about how you can use one. Allow me to briefly lay out some reasons sellers or buyers would want to use a lease option rather than a simple sale. Whether you find yourself on the lessee or lessor side of a lease option, knowing the advantages of both sides is best.

Owner/Seller/Lessor Benefits of a Lease Option

Lessee May Be Required to Perform Repairs – If so desired, with a lease option, the landlord will often require minor maintenance repairs to be the responsibility of the lessee (the tenant). After all, they plan on owning the property someday, so this added responsibility will help prepare them for that day. However, keep in mind that by shifting this responsibility to the lessee, many repairs may not be done properly or even done at all. I'm not telling you that you should or shouldn't ask this of your lessee—just understand that noncompliance *is* a possibility. If you are negotiating with a motivated seller to lease option his home to you, this can be a major benefit to explain to the seller.

Lease Option Tenants Tend to Treat Houses Better – Although this is not always 100% true, tenants who live in a home under the assumption they will soon own it will treat the property with more care than they would a typical rental. This might include higher craftsmanship in repairs, better cleaning, and more responsible choices (removing shoes on carpet, no drinks in the living room, etc.).

Incentive for Responsible Payments – Because the tenant may have paid a fairly hefty option fee to move in, they have extra incentive for paying rent on time and eventually buying the home. This will typically translate to more responsibility in performing properly.

No Agent Commission Upon Sale – Normally when you sell a house, the real estate agent fees can cost 6% or more. However, when a seller finds the buyer themselves without using an agent—as is the case with most lease option deals—the seller can avoid paying this fee, thereby saving thousands of dollars

Less Turnover and Fewer Turnover Costs – A lease option tenant typically has a different mind-set than a traditional tenant: they want to be buyers. This means they are far less likely to suddenly move out, and this means you have fewer vacancy expenses in your business. Additionally, if the tenant does move away, you have a security deposit as well as the option fee they paid at the beginning, so you won't lose as much money.

Possible Higher Sales Price – When you sell to a lease option buyer, they are typically less concerned with achieving the rock bottom prices that many traditional buyers seek. For those looking for a rent-to-own house, the price is far less important than the terms offered.

Tenant/Buyer Benefits of a Lease Option

While a lease option agreement offers some clear benefits for the lessor (owner), there are also numerous benefits for the lessee. Let's look at those now.

Ability to Lock In a Sales Price – If you recall, when a lease option is signed, part of the contract is an option to buy, which names a specific future purchase price on the property. This means that if a purchase price of $100,000 is agreed upon by the lessee and lessor, this price is locked in and cannot be changed if the tenant/buyer abides by the terms of the agreement and ends up purchasing the home. Even if the value of the home rises to $150,000, the tenant/buyer can purchase it for the predefined amount.

A Home to Call Their Own – Although the tenant may not be able to legally call the home their own, a lease option feels much more like a purchase than simply renting. This can give the tenant a feeling of security and pride of ownership.

A Plan for Home Ownership – Many tenants simply don't know the right way to begin to buy a home. A lease option allows them to "test drive" a home while creating a plan to actually purchase the property. From allowing them to learn how much they'll need for a down payment to giving them time to build their credit, a lease option can help guide a tenant into a home ownership.

Stability in the Home – Finally, by signing a lease option with a seller, a tenant has the ability to lock in a number of years in which the owner cannot legally sell the property to anyone else. This relieves the tenant of the fear that the owner may sell and kick them out, which is a common concern among tenants.

No Money Down Investing with a Lease Option

In this section, I'll finally explain some strategies for using a lease option to invest in real estate creatively. I hope you'll forgive me for the time spent explaining the intricacies of the lease option, but lease option investing is a fairly advanced method of investing, and doing so with creativity is even more complicated, so understanding the fundamentals before branching out is imperative.

If you don't yet feel comfortable with the concept, I invite you to read the first part of this chapter once more before continuing. However, if you are ready to move forward, let's continue.

As I mentioned earlier, as an investor, you may find yourself on either side of a lease option deal. In fact, there are at least four different strategies you could use as a creative investor. This section will cover all four and give examples of how they might work in the real world.

1. A Straight Lease Option (Lessor)

The most common way real estate investors use a lease option is by being the lessor, or owner, of the property. The investor finds a tenant-buyer and signs an agreement with them, giving them the right to buy the property in a specified time period for a defined price. Then, the investor either sells the property to that tenant-buyer or cycles through different tenant/buyers until one of them ultimately purchases the home.

Because the majority of lessees don't end up buying the home, the owner may end up renting to two, three, four, or even more different tenant/buyers before someone obtains a mortgage and buys the property. However, if you do some great screening ahead of time, hopefully, the first tenant you place will end up purchasing the property.

If more than one tenant/buyer is needed before the home actually sells, the benefit for the lessor, of course, is that each new tenant brings the opportunity to adjust the price to the house's current value as well as an additional option fee from the new tenant.

Although a lease option in this regard doesn't help you purchase the property creatively, this strategy can help you monetize by providing an exit strategy to one of the other creative finance techniques discussed in this book. In Chapter Ten, we'll spend a lot more time talking about how to combine different strategies for maximum creativity, and the lease option is definitely a powerful tool to pair with other methods.

Let's look at an example of how a straight lease option might look in the real world to an investor:

> Isaiah is just getting started with real estate investing and owns no properties except his primary residence. Isaiah decides to move, but rather than sell his home, he opts to carry out a lease option.
>
> He places an ad in the local paper and ends up signing a lease option with Carrie, a young urban professional who would love to buy a home but whose credit score is just a bit too low to qualify her for a typical mortgage. Carrie signs the lease, which states that she'll pay $900 per month in rent for the property, as well as the option agreement, which states that Carrie can choose to purchase the home for $119,000 at any time in the next three years. Carrie pays a $3,000 option fee plus a $900 security deposit and $900 for her first month's rent and moves in.
>
> After two years, Carrie has improved her credit rating enough to obtain a loan, so she fulfills her option contract and buys the house from Isaiah for $119,000. Isaiah thereby generated significant cash flow during those two years and was able to sell for top dollar with no sales commission to a real estate agent—a true win-win.

You may be thinking right now that an owner could use this strategy to take advantage of others by charging high fees to tenants who would never qualify anyway, churning through tenants with the full knowledge that they'll never end up buying. Yes, this does happen, but **I am adamantly opposed to such action**. We'll talk a bit more about this later in the "risks and downsides" section of this chapter, but understand that the lease option should be used only as a win-win solution for both parties, not as a method to collect more rent and put the tenant in a worse position than when they moved in. In addition to the ethical reason for this, there are some legal reasons taking advantage of tenants is just a bad idea, which I'll address shortly.

2. A Straight Lease Option (Lessee)

An investor can also acquire real estate using the lease option strategy by turning the tables and being on the other side of the deal—as the lessee. Although most owners probably would rather have cash, an owner may accept a lease option instead for a variety of reasons, especially if they are having a hard time selling their home. The investor and property owner would sign a lease option for the longest term and lowest rent possible, and the investor would then sublet the property to a tenant for the highest possible rent, keeping the cash flow difference.

When subletting property, such as in a lease option scenario like this, it is vital to let the lessor (owner) know what you plan to do. Don't try to hide anything—be open and honest about what you intend to do and explain the benefits for them in allowing you to do so. After all, the owner probably doesn't want to deal with tenants, drama, or any of the other issues that come with landlording, but as a real estate investor, this is your job! Essentially, you will act as a middleman, getting paid well without actually owning the property.

Additionally, because the investor has a signed, legal option to purchase the property at a specific price, the investor can market that property and potentially sell it in the future without even owning the property, because they can sell the option. (This is very similar to what a wholesaler does when they place a property under contract and then sell that contract to a cash buyer. I've dedicated an entire chapter to wholesaling later in this book, so don't worry about it now.) This is probably a little confusing, so let me illustrate this scenario with another example.

Reginald is a real estate investor with very little cash but a lot of creativity. He spends a significant amount of time looking for motivated sellers and eventually runs into Debbie, a homeowner who is struggling to sell her home. She went through a divorce and no longer needs the large home. She currently owes $215,000 on it, but its market value is barely $230,000, which doesn't leave her enough equity to pay a real estate agent.

Reginald and Debbie sign a lease option agreement so Reginald can take over the property and Debbie can move on with her life. Reginald agrees to pay $875 per month in rent with an option to purchase the home for $220,000 anytime within the next six years. He gives Debbie an option fee of $100 and takes control of the property.

Reginald then finds a tenant to rent the home for $1,475 per month, giving Reginald $600 per month in cash flow. He saves most of this cash flow, making sure he has enough to cover any future vacancies or repairs.

The market then climbs about 3% per year for the next five years, and the home is now worth $266,000, so Reginald finds a buyer to pay full price. This nets him close to $40,000 profit (not counting the five years of cash flow he collected) after he pays the closing costs—all for a $100 down deal that most investors would have passed up.

3. A Lease Option Sandwhich

The lease option sandwich is so named because it places you in two separate transactions on both sides of the deal—like the two slices of bread on your PB&J. First, you act as the lessee and find a property that you can lease option from the current owner. Next, you find a great tenant looking for a rent-to-own deal, and you sign a lease option with that tenant for the property. So there is a lease option on the front end of the deal and another lease option on the back end of the deal, and you are the peanut butter and jelly holding the "sandwich" together.

This strategy is very similar to the example above, but rather than finding any random buyer after five years, Reginald would actively seeks to rent the home to the same person who will end up buying it. Let's look at an example of how this lease option sandwich would work in the real world.

> Jerry is a motivated seller who has been transferred to another city for work but can't sell his current house, even though he has been trying for months. Real estate investor Kevin meets with Jerry and agrees to sign a five-year lease option agreement for $70,000, in which Kevin will pay Jerry $500 per month over those five years. Kevin gives Jerry an option fee of $1,000 and takes control of the property.
>
> Once the contract is signed, Kevin begins marketing for a tenant/buyer to sign a secondary lease option with. After a few days and a couple of Craigslist ads, Kevin makes an arrangement with a local graphic designer, Rhoda; she pays a $3,000 nonrefundable option fee, signs a two-year lease with a two-year option to buy the home for $100,000, and agrees to pay a monthly rent of $1,000.

At this point, Kevin is simply the middleman. Rhoda pays Kevin $1,000 each and every month, while Kevin pays Jerry $500 per month, giving Kevin a monthly cash flow of $500. Additionally, Rhoda put down a $3,000 option fee, whereas Kevin gave Jerry only $1,000 for the option fee, which means Kevin is not only making significant monthly cash flow but he also made $2,000 on the deal. (However, if Rhoda ends up buying the property, that $2,000 will come off the top of what Kevin would get at closing. He is smart and saves that $2,000 for a rainy day.)

Two years later, Rhoda decides *not* to buy the home. She moves out, forfeiting her $3,000 option fee, and Kevin (with three years left on his five-year lease option contract) decides to look for another tenant/buyer. He finds Sam, a local bank teller, who pays a $3,000 option fee and moves into the property, paying $1,100 per month for rent and getting an option to purchase the home for $110,000. After one year, Sam is able to qualify for a mortgage, completing his option and paying $110,000 for the property. Kevin sends all the paperwork to the local title company who carries out the sale, and he walks away from the deal with almost $40,000—in addition to the cash flow he had been receiving for months.

What Happens After the Contract Time Expires?

In this example, Kevin first signed a five-year lease option with the homeowner, Jerry. Luckily, Kevin's second tenant ultimately purchased the property at the end of year three. But what if he hadn't? After all, the majority of tenant/buyers never actually end up carrying out their option. So what if Kevin's initial contract with Jerry runs out?

All is not lost; at this point, Kevin would have a few options:

1. Kevin could ask Jerry for an extension, perhaps another five years. Jerry has been renting the home to Kevin for five years anyway, so Kevin could simply request to continue the process. You'll never know if you don't ask.

2. Kevin could sell the home to a retail buyer. Remember, Kevin had a lease option to purchase the home from Jerry for $70,000. He could search out a buyer, perhaps even listing the property on the multiple listing service (MLS), and try to assign the contract to a retail home buyer. He could even do some cosmetic improvements to help the home sell faster.

3. Kevin could sell to an investor, even at a discount. If Kevin got a good deal on the home from Jerry, he may be able to sell the home to a cash buyer, like a local investor, who wants to use the home as a rental. Even if Kevin doesn't get the full market value of the home, as long as he can sell it for more than his option price, he can make a profit.

4. Kevin could decline to purchase the property and split from Jerry. Remember, Kevin only has an *option* to buy the property, not an obligation. Jerry would get the home back, and because the market has probably improved over the five-year period, he may be able get much more than the $70,000 he was planning to receive from Kevin. If not, at least Jerry's mortgage has been paid down, and he's no worse off than he was when he started the whole process.

One of the reasons I like the lease option sandwich so much is that it can truly be a win-win-win for everyone involved, if it is structured correctly. To return to our example with Jerry and Kevin,

- Jerry was relieved of the burden of dealing with his property and the payment.
- Jerry received the fair price he was comfortable with.
- Kevin was able to make great monthly income and a significant profit with little to no money out of pocket.
- Sam is able to buy his dream house and obtain long-term financing.

Don't you just love win-win-win situations?

Tips for a Successful Lease Option Sandwich

Here are seven tips for making sure that your lease option sandwich goes off without any major issues and that you are able to achieve the most security, income, and fairness for everyone possible.

1. The longer your contract is with the homeowner, the better. Three years is better than one, five is better than three, and ten is better than five. The more time you have, the more options you have. Also, ensure that your contract with your tenant/buyer is shorter than your contract with the owner/ seller. You don't want to offer your tenant/buyer a five-year lease but sign just a three-year lease with the owner.

2. Always let the owner know what you are doing. This is not a strategy you should ever think of using without having everyone on the same page. Don't pretend you'll be living in the home just to get the contract, only to turn around and sublet it to the tenant. Be up front and honest, and make everyone comfortable with the arrangement. Your job as a real estate investor is to solve problems, so do that!

3. Screen well! Screening your tenant is one of the most important steps you can take to ensure a positive landlording experience, especially with a lease option sandwich. Although tenant-screening

practices are beyond the scope of this book, the most important things you can do are as follows:

- **Always run a background check on your tenant.** Look for evictions, criminal activities, etc.
- **Make sure the tenant/buyer has good enough credit.** Their credit score doesn't need to be 800 for them to qualify, but it needs to be reasonable/improvable for them to be able to get a mortgage to cash you out eventually.
- **Look for stability.** A tenant who moves every six months without reason is probably not a great candidate.
- **Don't discriminate.** Doing so could land you in jail, so know your local and federal discrimination laws and adhere to them.

For more information on how to do screen tenants, be sure to read the free, in-depth article "Tenant Screening: The Ultimate Guide"[32] from BiggerPockets.

4. Connect and qualify your tenant/buyer with a mortgage professional, also known as an RMLO—short for residential mortgage lenders and originator. This individual can sit down with your potential tenant and explain what they need to do to qualify for a loan, to make sure they can reasonably hope to actually qualify. A good mortgage professional can work with your tenant/buyer to create a credit road map to help guide them from where they are now to being able to qualify for a mortgage. Setting up a meeting between the tenant/buyer and your favorite mortgage professional is helpful for both the tenant/buyer and you, and it can also help prove that you are not trying to take advantage of a tenant

---

[32] http://www.biggerpockets.com/tenantscreening

if you are ever accused of such.

5. Arrange to pay the owner's mortgage for him. After all, you don't want to send the owner a payment each month and suddenly find out the bank is foreclosing on the property because the owner decided to pocket the money rather than passing it on to the bank.

6. Legally record your option contract with the owner at your county administrative department. By legally recording the option contract, you will put a "cloud" on the title, and the owner will not be able to sell the property until it's cleared. If you do not record the contract, the owner might decide to sell to another investor or a retail buyer, and your only recourse would be a very expensive and stressful lawsuit. Recording can usually be done for less than $100 and normally requires only that the agreement be signed and notarized.

7. *Don't* apply any portion of the rent toward the tenant/buyer's future down payment. This was a popular method of doing lease options in the past, but since the SAFE Act and Dodd-Frank legislation were passed, there has been legal concern on the part of many investors that portions of rent applied toward the tenant's future down payment constitutes a "security," which means many additional rules and regulations must be followed (ones you don't want to deal with). Additionally, most banks will not allow this credit anyway, so it's just best to make the rent the rent.

8. Don't be a jerk. Do you remember the scene from *Spider-Man* where Uncle Ben states, "With great power comes great responsibility?" By this point, you can probably see that there is a lot of potential power in the lease option sandwich, but this same advice that guides Spider-Man should guide you as well, because with lease options, one could very easily be a jerk and take advantage of tenants.

For me, this is one of the biggest concerns for someone

looking to engage in a lease option agreement. Because the vast majority of lease option tenants never end up actually purchasing the home, the lessee may be primed for failure from the beginning. Many lease option investors know this and proactively take steps to make it nearly impossible for the lessee to ever close on the deal. They charge huge up-front fees for a totally unqualified tenant to move in, give them a short time frame in which to buy, kick them out, and then repeat the process. The tenant, on the other hand, ends up in a far worse financial position than they were in originally. I believe this kind of unethical behavior is what gives the real estate investing industry a bad name. Don't add to the problem.

Treat your lease option agreements as a chance to create a win-win-win scenario and help others get what they want as well. Use your power for good, not evil. This means only entering a lease option with tenants who could very reasonably obtain a loan within several years, without charging an exorbitant option fee. I want to be fair and have all parties happy with how things turned out at the end of the transaction, whether the tenant officially buys the property or not.

Finally, the government knows this is a problem and frowns on landlords who take advantage of people. The SAFE Act and Dodd-Frank legislations were enacted, in part, to help deal with these problems. Not only can you give landlords a bad name, but you could wind up in prison. Don't be a jerk.

4. A Master Lease Option

The fourth strategy I want to share with you is known as a master lease option, or MLO. An MLO takes the lease option concept to a whole new level, and its use can have a tremendous impact on your real estate investing, especially if you are trying to invest creatively.

An MLO works pretty much the same way as a regular lease option, in that there is a lease, a lessor, a lessee, and an option fee. However, with an MLO, the lessee (the tenant/buyer) generally pays all the expenses associated with the property, including taxes, insurance, and any maintenance concerns—and then sublets the property out to tenants who then live in the property.

Although an MLO can be used with any size property, it is most common with larger investments, such as apartment buildings and commercial real estate. It is very similar to seller financing, which we'll cover in the next chapter, but no title is actually transferred. Instead, the property is simply leased for a long period of time for a set monthly rental amount. The owner (the lessor) receives monthly payments but is no longer involved in managing the property. Instead, the investor who has the option (the lessee) takes care of the property, collecting rent, paying the bills, and acting as the proxy owner, keeping the cash flow difference.

An MLO can be a great way to buy a large multifamily or commercial property using very little money out of pocket. Because you are not actually purchasing the property, there is no change in title, but you are entitled to all the cash flow (positive or negative), as well as any appreciation benefits, because you lock in a future purchase price as part of the option contract.

Let me give you an example of how an MLO might work in the real world.

Marsha was a 20-something investor with a few house flips and rentals under her belt who was looking to invest in larger properties. After reading several books on the subject, she decided investing in apartment complexes was the path she would take in her investment career. She mentioned her ambitions to a local investor, Phil, at church the following Sunday. "Actually," Phil said, "I'm looking to travel more and sell off my own apartment complex." This is networking at its finest!

After several conversations, Marsha and Phil agreed to work together to accomplish both of their goals. Being a 20-something investor, Marsha had very little money, so giving Phil enough to even pay the closing costs was beyond her capabilities. Instead, they decided to start with an MLO. Phil agreed to accept a monthly rent of $2,500 and to give Marsha three years in which to purchase the property. Paperwork was signed, and Marsha took over the property with no cash out of pocket, and with cash flowing from day one.

Marsha's job was then to manage the property, accept rent, manage any handymen, and pay all the bills—100% of them. Meanwhile, Phil and his wife bought a camper and began enjoying their retirement, driving around the United States and loving the steady MLO payment deposited in their account each and every month.

If this story seems too good to be true, I have a secret: this is the story of how I bought my 24-unit apartment building when I was just 25 years old. (I had to change the name and gender, of course, to throw you off!) We later converted the master lease option to a full-blown seller-financed deal (we'll cover these in the next chapter). So these kinds of opportunities *do* exist and can be done for very little money out of pocket. Notice that the deal came to me because I simply learned about the concept and told other people about my passions. I had no idea that "Phil" owned an apartment complex; I just let my passion spill over into my day-to-day life.

As I've said before, networking is a lifestyle.

The same can happen for you, and amazing deals can fall into your lap if you take the time to educate yourself and share your dreams with others. You never know what you might find.

Risks and Drawbacks of the Lease Option

1. The Due-on-Sale Clause – You've probably heard about the dreaded due-on-sale clause before, but just so we're all on the same page, let me give you a brief description of what it is. In nearly every mortgage paperwork, there is a paragraph that sounds something like this:

I. If the trustor shall sell, convey, or alienate said property, or any part thereof, or any interest therein, or shall be divested of his title or any interest therein in any manner of way, whether voluntarily or involuntarily, without the written consent of the beneficiary being first had and obtained, beneficiary shall have the right, at its option, or declare any indebtedness or obligations secured hereby, irrespective of the maturity date specified in any note evidencing the same, immediately due and payable.

This clause declares that the mortgage holder—the lender—has the legal right to demand to be paid back, in full, if the property is sold. If this happens, and the borrower cannot pay back the entire loan in full, the lender could foreclose and reclaim the property. Not cool.

"But Brandon," you say, "we never bought or sold the property! This is just a lease with an option to buy." Very smart, and very true. Nevertheless, some people worry that a lease option could entice a bank to call the note due, based on the due-on-sale clause. In the lender's mind, they may argue that although the legal title was not transferred with the lease option, "equitable interest" in the property has been transferred.

Furthermore, many due-on-sale clauses specifically note "lease options" as a condition for the due-on-sale to be exercised, in which case it's pretty black and white (literally). I just took a look at my own primary residence mortgage, and sure enough, it states that a lease option can trigger the due-on-sale clause. I would wager most of my loans have something similar.

Is any of this likely? How fearful of the due-on-sale clause should you be? Will the bank really come and demand payment from you?

At least in the past, banks have generally ignored the issue, and I've never even heard of a case where a note was called due because of a lease option. However, the possibility does exist, so I must mention it and make sure you are aware of any potential problems.

There are additional concerns that by breaking the due-on-sale clause without notifying the bank, you are breaching an ethical code and possibly even breaking mortgage law.

So what can you do to prevent this kind of thing from happening? The main way is to have a great deal. If there is a ton of equity in the deal, chances are good that you could sell quickly or try to work something out. Or simply don't do a deal that involves a due-on-sale clause.

Creative finance is about finding solutions, not forcing them.

Furthermore, at BiggerPockets, we recommend *never* going behind your lender's back. Therefore, if the mortgage paperwork specifically forbids lease options, you probably shouldn't do one with that property unless you are 100% comfortable with the risk—and you are not putting the seller at any undue risk. Plenty of other strategies in this book could work just as well. Creative finance is about finding solutions, not forcing them.

While the due-on-sale clause is definitely a concern with lease options, it's not the only one, so let's move on to some more risks to keep in mind.

2. Major Repairs the Owner Can't Cover – A second problem that could arise is repairs, especially if you are the lessor in a lease option scenario and you are renting out a property to tenants. As I mentioned earlier, you could require the tenant to cover repairs under a certain amount, and in theory, this arrangement is great. However, certain issues could come up that you need to be aware of.

For example, what if a large repair is needed that your tenant can't afford, such as a furnace failure? Who will pay for that? Hopefully, your legal contract with the owner will spell out exactly who is responsible, and you could take legal action if absolutely necessary.

Additionally, a great suggestion from John Jackson[33], a lease option expert on BiggerPockets.com, is to pay for a home warranty on the property (or have the tenants pay for one) at the start of the lease option, one that covers all major maintenance problems on the home. These policies tend to be less than $500 and can be a life saver when the furnace does blow up.

3. Changing Legislation – Finally, the lease option world is changing, and it's severely unsettling right now as to where things are headed. Most of the changes and uncertainty have come about because of passing of the SAFE Act and the Dodd-Frank legislation since the housing collapse several years ago. These reforms were enacted to prevent a similar meltdown in our economy, but much of the language designed for big banks and huge corporations also seems to apply to small-time investors like you and me. No one is sure where things will end up or what actually applies to small investors, so the uncertainty also creates a

---

[33] http://www.biggerpockets.com/users/LeasingToBuy

degree of risk. Be sure to stick close to BiggerPockets as we continue to monitor developments in this rapidly changing industry.

Lease Options Wrap-Up

I hope you can see the tremendous possibilities available with a lease option, especially for those with more creativity than cash. Entire books have been written on the subject of lease options, so the past several thousand words cannot be considered the only guide on how to successfully execute them. If this is a strategy you plan on using, I highly recommend you learn more and study up on how to make them work in your market. Find someone on BiggerPockets.com who currently works in the lease option niche and ask questions!

Lease options are not an easy beginner strategy, as many of the real estate gurus might have you believe, but they can work for you if you take the steps necessary to learn how to properly apply them. If you want to get into buy-and-hold landlording, it can be a great way to do so without needing to get bank financing, save up a huge down payment, or wait months for a loan to go through. However, there are risks involved and some ethical questions you need to fully understand before moving forward.

In the next chapter, we'll talk about a similar strategy—*seller financing*—and discuss how to use the owner of a property to invest in real estate with little to no money out of pocket.

CHAPTER EIGHT: SELLER FINANCING

One of the most popular methods of using little or no money down when investing in real estate is *seller financing*.

Perhaps the oldest of the creative options outlined in this book, seller financing has become less and less popular in recent years because of the increase in availability of "easy credit" and record low mortgage rates. However, knowing how to effectively use seller financing in your business can help you get more deals done faster and for less money.

Additionally, mortgage rates are rising, so by learning how to master seller financing today, not only are you adding a tool to your toolbox of financing options, but you are also preparing

147

yourself for the day when seller financing becomes more popular once again.

What Is Seller Financing?

Seller financing is just what it sounds like: the seller provides the financing. In other words, the owner of the property acts as the bank, and although legal ownership of the property changes hands, the payment is sent directly to the previous owner, rather than to a bank, for a specific duration and with a defined monthly payment.

For example, I may want to purchase a rental house, but I do not want or am unable to get traditional bank financing. The seller would like $100,000 for the property but is willing to "carry the contract" (aka "carry paper"), which is investor jargon for when someone agrees to finance a property (or part of the property) they currently own so the buyer doesn't need to get external financing from a lender. In this case, the owner would ask for $5,000 down and a 10% interest rate on the remaining $95,000 amortized over 30 years, for a monthly payment of $833.69, before taxes and insurance. I'd agree to his terms and after doing my due diligence, I would close on the property through my local title company. I'd then look for a tenant who would rent the home for $1,600 per month and collect the cash flow difference each month.

In this scenario, the seller gets a great interest rate on their money, I get to buy the house for just $5,000 down, and I don't have to deal with a bank at all. Seller financing can be another great win-win for all parties involved. But what's the catch?

Why aren't these arrangements more popular?

The Problem with Seller Financing

One major problem with seller financing puts a wrench in the whole strategy for the millions of American homes that currently carry a mortgage: the due-on-sale clause. We talked about this clause in the previous chapter when I outlined the risks of a lease option, but allow me to repeat the gist of it: the due-on-sale clause is a legal part of nearly every mortgage paperwork that gives the bank the right to demand that the loan be paid back in full, immediately, if the property is sold (hence the name "due on sale").

So you can see the core problem with seller financing: in such an arrangement, the property is being sold. In other words, if there is a mortgage on a property, and the property is sold using seller financing, then the bank could come and demand to be paid back in full that moment or it could foreclose.

Will that actually happen?

Well, remember that the due-on-sale clause gives the bank the *right* to demand full payment; it doesn't *require* the bank to do so. The bank may be perfectly accepting of the arrangement and never say a word. However, the risk you carry is great whenever you sell a property that has a due-on-sale clause. If the bank does demand full payment immediately and you can't pay the bank the entire loan balance, the property may be foreclosed on. If you are buying from a homeowner, the homeowner may get foreclosed on, and both of you would lose the property. Obviously, this is not a situation you want to find yourself in. There is one simple solution:

Only use seller financing when the seller owns the home free and clear (i.e., when the seller has no loans on the property).

Literally millions of properties are prime for you to buy using seller financing.

In other words, if you truly want to eliminate the risk of being foreclosed on for violating the due-on-sale clause, don't use seller financing to buy a home unless the existing loan is first paid off. Your goal when using seller financing is to find sellers who don't have a mortgage. Although this may seem difficult, the *Los Angeles Times* reports that 29.3% of American homeowners do not have a mortgage on their property.[34] Therefore, literally *millions* of properties are prime for you to buy using seller financing.

Why Buy Using Seller Financing?

Seller financing offers numerous benefits, so let's look at a few of the most common:

1. Ease of Financing – As mentioned earlier, when you use pure seller financing to purchase a property, you avoid having to use a bank, which can mean the difference between a deal and no deal for many people. If you are tapped out on the number of mortgages you can get, seller financing can be a great tool in your toolbox to obtain additional rental property.

2. Possible No or Low Down Payments – Because you are dealing directly with a homeowner seller, there are no cut-and-dry rules regarding the down payment. You aren't dealing with rigid rules imposed by Fannie Mae or Freddie Mac, which require 20%–30% down on an investment property. Instead, you get what you negotiate with the seller. The seller may want nothing down, or they may want 50%, but you won't know until you ask and negotiate.

3. Option for Creativity in Structuring the Deal – As I mentioned earlier, the rules when dealing with banks can be extremely rigid, but this is not the case with seller financing. Seller financing allows you to get creative to solve a problem. Rates, terms, the payment amount, payment dates, and everything else is completely negotiable, which can turn a mediocre deal into a great

---

[34] http://articles.latimes.com/2013/jan/10/business/la-fi-free-and-clear-20130110

deal.

4. Purchase "Unfinanceable" Properties – Sometimes, the condition of a property may be too poor to allow you to use traditional financing. In these cases, seller financing can give the buyer a chance to own the property, begin fixing it up, and possibly refinance into a more traditional form of financing down the road (or never—the possibilities are numerous!).

5. Doesn't Show on Your Credit Report – Unless the seller of the home signs up with one of the credit reporting agencies to report the debt (very unlikely), chances are your seller financed deal will not end up on your credit report. This can make obtaining other loans and mortgages in the future much easier.

There are, no doubt, numerous other reasons you may want to use seller financing, so don't be afraid to seek out opportunities where you can apply it. It truly can be a great way to finance properties of any size. However, if it's so good for the buyer, does a seller have good reasons to agree to it?

Why Would Sellers Sell Via Seller Financing?

If I gave you the choice between getting $100 today or $1 per month for the next 30 years, which would you take? Most of you would want the $100 right now, but if you do the math, $1 per month for 30 years is $360, which is more than three times the lump sum of $100. Still want the $100?

Perhaps.

Some of you reading would take the $1 a month, whereas others would take the lump sum. It all comes down to personal choice.

The same principle this question demonstrates is true for

home sellers. Many homeowners who own their house free and clear would rather take the cash and move on. However, for a large number of sellers, the value of getting monthly payments outweighs the need for a large lump-sum check. Let's look more closely at why owners might choose to sell via seller financing rather than just getting cashed out.

1. Monthly Income – Perhaps the most common reason sellers would prefer to sell via seller financing is to get monthly income. As in the $100 or $1 per month example I used, a lot of individuals would simply prefer to steadily receive checks each month instead of one lump sum. This is especially true for older sellers on a fixed income who need stable monthly income to survive and pay the bills. A $100,000 chunk of money would last only so long for a seller, but if that income were financed over 30 years, the money would last them much further into retirement.

2. Better ROI – Many homeowners choose to sell with seller financing because the interest they get from the financing is greater than they would likely get elsewhere. For example, if a homeowner were to sell a home for $100,000, they could put that money into a certificate of deposit at the bank and receive 1.5% annual percentage yield, or they could seller finance their home and get 6%, 8%, or more.

Many seasoned real estate investors understand this concept and eventually move their portfolio from a "holding" phase to a "selling" phase, using seller financing to avoid the hassle of being an owner, while still collecting monthly income by carrying the contract. Therefore, some of the best possible candidates for seller financing are other real estate investors who are changing their strategy. (On a side note, this is another reason making friends with as many local real estate investors as you can is so important. When they are ready to get out of the landlord game, they may choose to sell to you and carry the contract in the process.)

3. Spread Out Taxes – Anytime you make money, the government wants its share, and when you sell real estate, it's no different. This issue may not be as important for homeowners, because of the IRS rule that allows homeowners to avoid paying taxes on up to $500,000 in profit from selling their primary residence, as long as it meets certain specific criteria.

However, real estate investors are not so lucky and are must pay taxes when they sell. For example, if an investor spends 30 years paying off a rental property mortgage and now owns the home free and clear, and he decides to sell the property for $100,000, that investor would need to pay taxes on that gain, which could result in a hefty tax bill.

Therefore, many investors choose to sell using seller financing rather than getting a lump sum, to spread out most of those tax payments over the life of the loan on the seller financed property. You see, the IRS has special tax rules for installment sales, such as ones using seller financing, so the seller may need to pay only a small portion of that tax bill each year while the loan is being paid off. Be sure to talk to a CPA for more details on this.

4. Can't Sell Otherwise – As I mentioned in the previous section, many properties simply are not sellable to a typical bank-financed borrower because they are in such poor condition. Seller financing can allow the seller to unload such a property without needing to fix it up first.

Example of a Seller-Financed Deal

So how does seller financing work in the real world? The following is an example of how you might structure a seller-financed deal to create a win-win for all parties involved. Keep in mind that this is not legal advice; this is just an example of how one investor structured a purchase.

153

Paul owned a nice triplex in the suburbs of Chicago. He purchased the property with all cash ten years earlier and has now decided it's time to retire and began looking at his options. Paul knows the property is worth approximately $250,000, and if he tries to sell it through a real estate agent, he'll spend $15,000 in commissions and another $10,000 in seller-assisted closing costs, netting him $225,000. However, after paying taxes, he'd likely have only around $150,000 remaining, which he may be able to earn 8% on in the stock market.

Instead, Paul talks with Samantha, an up-and-coming real estate investor excited to get her first property. Samantha had been learning from Paul for several months and built a great relationship with him. So Paul sells Samantha the property for $250,000 with just $3,000 down to cover closing costs and an 8% interest-only loan on that $250,000. Paul now makes $20,000 per year from the property, 100% passively, while Samantha owns and manages the property and collects the cash flow every month.

Partial Seller Financing

Up to this point, I've discussed seller financing mostly from an "entirety" position, meaning that the entire property is sold using seller financing. However, seller financing lets you get your creative juices flowing. One such creative way to use seller financing is known as *partial seller financing*.

What if a seller doesn't own their home free and clear but does have some good equity in it? What if the owner has 50% equity in his home, or 90%?

This kind of situation allows you to let the seller finance just part of the deal, while a traditional lender finances the other part. This can get a little bit confusing, so let's look at an example.

Charlie owns his home, which is currently for sale for $100,000, but he owes only $50,000 to the bank on his mortgage.

Susan is a buy-and-hold investor who is looking to buy Charlie's property, but she doesn't have the large down payment needed for a conventional mortgage.

So, Susan works a partial seller financed arrangement with Charlie and her lender in which the bank provides a $65,000 first mortgage, Charlie agrees to "carryback" a second mortgage for $30,000, and Susan can put just $5,000 down. The $65,000 goes to pay off the original $50,000 loan of Charlie's, and he ends up with $15,000 in cash plus a "note" (mortgage) for $30,000, giving him some monthly income for the next X number of years.

Don't worry if that was confusing, this is pretty advanced stuff! The point is, seller financing allows for some creativity, and using a seller's equity to partially fund a real estate deal is a path you may want to take some day.

Keep in mind, however, that many banks and lending institutions do not allow sellers to carryback second mortgages anymore (this was much more common in the past) and may require you to still put a down payment into the deal, no matter how much the seller agrees to carry. However, you won't know until you pick up the phone and start asking different lenders what their rules are.

Three Ways to Find Seller-Financed Deals

So you now have a pretty good idea of how seller financing works and how you can use it in your real estate investing to get more deals. But how do you find owners who are willing to carry the contract and provide seller financing? Here are three simple ways to find these sellers:

1. Ask – It may seem obvious, but sometimes all it takes is a simple question. When talking with sellers, whether directly or through your real estate agent, simply ask the question, "Do you need to be 100% cashed out, or are you able to provide any seller financing?"

As I hope I have made clear, seller financing is about creating a win-win situation, not trying to take advantage of someone. Therefore, never be afraid to ask about seller financing, because the seller may be ecstatic to provide it but had just never thought of it before. Besides, it never hurts to ask. What's the worst they can say?

2. Look for Keywords – When scanning the MLS, Craigslist, and other sources for finding properties, keep an eye out for phrases such as "owner will carry," "owc," "flexible terms," "seller financing," and "motivated" as well as any other indication that the seller is open to a conversation about seller financing.

3. Direct Mail – Although we will cover this later when we talk about wholesaling in Chapter Ten, understand that you can purchase lists of homeowners that specify how much equity the homeowner has in their property. Although the list companies, such as ListSource,[35] don't always get the numbers correct, you can at least begin to market to individuals who probably have a good deal of equity in their properties. Significant equity is a good sign that seller financing may be a possibility, so when sending out direct mail, keep an eye out for high equity, and again, don't be afraid to ask.

---

[35] http://www.listsource.com

Risks and Drawbacks of Seller Financing

Seller financing can provide some excellent options for you as a buyer, but the strategy is not without some risks and dangers. This section will outline three of the most common concerns when dealing with seller financing and offer some tips on overcoming those potential problems.

1. The Due-on-Sale Clause – We've covered this topic quite a bit already, but I can't help but rehash it here. It's vitally important that you understand what the due-on-sale clause is and why it matters. You don't want to endanger the seller's credit or your relationship with a seller by trying to circumvent this clause. Understand that if you buy a home using seller financing and the home has a mortgage with a due-on-sale clause, the bank may foreclose on the seller, leaving both of you in a financial mess.

Again, the simplest solution is to use seller financing only on properties that are owned free and clear. The one exception I would have to this rule (maybe, in certain situations) is for very short-term financing. Some investors out there use seller financing with existing mortgages (often called a "wrap," because you wrap one mortgage over another) despite the due-on-sale clause, because they believe they can quickly fix the property up and either sell or refinance before the bank finds out and has an issue. I won't tell you this is a great idea; I'll leave that for you to decide based on your risk tolerance level.

2. Higher Interest Rates – Although seller financing allows for incredible creativity, generally speaking, you will pay a higher than normal rate with seller financing. This has not always been the case, but in today's lending environment, with loan rates under 4%, getting a seller to accept an interest rate as low as that is difficult (though some investors do negotiate 0% interest seller financed loans). Just be sure to run the numbers with the interest rates you plan on obtaining, and make sure they work for the deal.

3. Fewer Potential Properties – Let's face it, even though seller financing can be a great win-win for both parties, the vast majority of homeowners are either unable (because of existing mortgages) or unwilling to carry a contract and provide seller financing. Therefore, the pool of potential deals is significantly smaller when you are looking to work with seller financing. But don't let this discourage you! As I mentioned earlier, approximately 30% of the homes in America do not have a mortgage and could be great options for seller financing.

Seller Financing Doesn't Mean "Buy a Bad Deal"

Before we move on from the topic of seller financing, I want to make something very clear: although seller financing allows you to obtain properties without using a bank, this does not give you an excuse to overpay for a property.

Many real estate investors like to sell using seller financing because they can charge a premium for the property. However, you should not pay a premium. Leverage is only leverage when used responsibly; otherwise, it simply becomes a liability.

So go out there, add the seller financing tool to your toolbox, and go make some magic happen.

In the next chapter, we'll talk about the longest and perhaps most complicated method in this book: *wholesaling.* Although wholesaling is a completely different animal from the other methods discussed thus far, I believe learning to be an expert wholesaler will help you in every aspect of your real estate investing efforts. So whether or not you ever plan to wholesale a deal, pay close attention to the next chapter. Wholesaling could become a valuable tool in your investor toolbox.

CHAPTER NINE: REAL ESTATE WHOLESALING

I was reluctant to write this chapter.

Not because I don't like wholesaling—I do—but because I see so many people **fail** at it. Day after day, people come to us at BiggerPockets and say, "I want to be a wholesaler!" but two weeks later, they are gone, and I never hear from them again.

Why? Honestly, I don't know. But I have some guesses:

- "Experts" make it sound really easy—when it's not.
- People think it takes no money (well...).
- It's more complicated than they thought.
- It takes more time than they thought.
- They get bored.

For whatever reason, people interested in wholesaling tend to suddenly disappear from the real estate scene. However, the simple fact is that wholesaling is one of the most popular methods for newbies who want to get involved with real estate investing, and nothing I say or do will change that.

What I *can* do is make succeeding easier for those interested in this option by providing the best resource possible for being a real estate wholesaler. I believe that if more people realized what the whole picture looked like, they would stick with it and find success. If you are interested in making money by wholesaling real estate, I encourage you to take your time and really dig into this chapter. Take notes, highlight sections, teach others what you are learning, and perhaps most importantly, head to the BiggerPockets Wholesaling Forums[36] and start interacting with some successful wholesalers.

I hope that this chapter will provide you with an exhaustive overview of wholesaling and that you'll be able to incorporate it into your strategy to invest in real estate with little to no money down.

Important: This chapter is about far more than just wholesaling. This chapter is first and foremost about marketing and finding great deals, so even if you *never* plan to wholesale a deal, I encourage you to read through it anyway. I believe wholesaling can be a valuable tool in an investor's toolbox, so learning the basics will serve you well in your quest to become a creative real estate investor.

With that said, let's get going. We'll start at the beginning, because as Julie Andrews tells me, "It's a very good place to start."

---

[36] https://www.biggerpockets.com/forums/93-wholesaling

What Is Real Estate Wholesaling?

A few years ago, I wanted to start a jeans company. My plan was simple: create an online website that sold jeans for tall and thin men like me, because I can't find jeans that fit, and I know a lot of other tall/thin men have the same problem. In my efforts to start this venture, I realized that I would be the retailer—the "front end"— from whom customers would purchase the jeans. Somewhere in China, Malaysia, India, Mexico, or elsewhere, hundreds of factory workers (the manufacturer) would stitch together the denim to make the jeans.

However, I don't speak the language of any of those countries, and I don't know a whole lot about jeans. I needed help. Enter the wholesaler. A wholesaler is the middleman who connects the retailer to the product source, collecting a fee for doing so.

Wholesalers typically buy in bulk, for cheap, and sell for a higher price to a retailer. This business process is the same in the clothing industry, the meat industry, the construction industry, and almost every other industry that sells to the general public. For example, Home Depot can't simply call up a factory in Bangladesh and order more toilets. You need a middleman, and the wholesaler is that man (or woman).

A real estate wholesaler finds deals and connects a retail buyer (typically an investor) with those deals, charging a fee for doing so. A wholesaler is trained to market for those good deals, negotiate the best discount, put together a solid contract, and then sell at a markup to someone else who is not trained or prepared to do this.

But I'm getting ahead of myself. Let me take a step back and walk you through how a wholesale deal typically plays out from start to finish, because the process can be a little confusing for someone not familiar with it. I find it helpful to see the terrain at an altitude of 20,000 feet before blazing through the jungle, so consider this your flyover (keep in mind that there are *many* different techniques for wholesaling a property, and we will cover those in this chapter, but this example is just one of the more popular options):

- **Step One:** Find a great deal from a motivated seller.
- **Step Two:** Negotiate a great price that makes financial sense to both parties.
- **Step Three:** Sign a "purchase and sale agreement" with the seller.
- **Step Four:** Find a cash buyer (house flipper, landlord, etc.).
- **Step Five:** Legally connect the cash buyer to the motivated seller.
- **Step Six:** Collect the difference in price between what the seller's contract is for and what the cash buyer will pay.
- **Step Seven:** Rinse and Repeat with more and more deals!

If you found this difficult to follow, don't worry; it's confusing for most people the first time they hear it. Stay with me, and this will all make perfect sense soon.

Example of a Wholesale Deal

Let me walk you through an example of a fairly typical wholesale deal. I'll use this example throughout this chapter, so don't be concerned if you don't understand every aspect right away. This is the completed puzzle, but after I have presented the whole thing, I'll dive into the details of each piece.

Beth is a new wholesaler looking for her first deal and using a variety of smart marketing techniques. She gets a phone call about a three-bedroom, two-bath, 1,400 square foot home at 123 Main Street in a fairly desirable neighborhood. The owner, Clarence, has been trying to sell on his own—with no luck. Beth talks with Clarence and discovers that he is making two house payments and cannot afford both, so he is getting very motivated to sell. However, the house is painted an ugly purple, has outdated carpet, and smells like the four German Shepherds that have lived there for a decade. No one is interested in the house in its current condition. Clarence does not have the funds necessary to get the home into marketable condition. Besides, he's just tired of dealing with it and wants out. Clarence is stuck.

Beth knows the neighborhood well and has done her homework. There have been a dozen sales of similar homes (all fixed up) in the neighborhood in the previous six months, ranging from $135,000 to $175,000. Being conservative, Beth estimates the home's value, if the place is all fixed up, at around $143,000, but she knows it needs about $20,000 worth of repairs. Clarence has been asking $120,000, but because of the condition of the property, no one will even bother to look at it.

Beth builds a good rapport with Clarence, does the math, and offers him $74,500 for the property. She lets Clarence know that either she or a business associate of hers will buy the home within six weeks, and Clarence will no longer have the double payment. After some minor negotiation, Clarence accepts the offer, and the two of them sign a contract for Beth (or her business associate) to purchase the property.

Beth thanks Clarence and immediately calls Jackson, a local house flipper she met via the BiggerPockets Forums. She tells Jackson about the deal and gives him the address. He and Beth go look at the house together, and Jackson agrees to pay $84,500 for the home. Beth then "assigns" the contract to Jackson for a

$10,000 fee to be paid at closing, collecting a $2,000 nonrefundable deposit up front from Jackson.

Several weeks later, Jackson and Clarence sign all the paperwork at their local title company. Clarence receives the $74,500 Beth offered him, Jackson pays $84,500 for the property, which he intends to rehab and resell for a profit, and Beth receives her $10,000 wholesaling fee and moves on to the next deal—after enjoying a night at the local steakhouse to celebrate!

This deal is an idealized wholesale deal, and it has obviously been simplified. However, while wholesaling is not as easy as the gurus might make it out to be, it's not an impossible task either.

Wholesaling, at its core, is about solving problems. In the example, the owner, Clarence, had a problem, and Beth made a fee by solving his problem, just as a real estate agent would by solving a retail seller's problems.

Personally, I used to dislike wholesaling because I thought, "Well, isn't it wrong to try to steal properties from people?"

Yes, it is wrong to steal. Don't do it.

However, ethical wholesaling is not about stealing anything. Again, it's about solving problems and helping people. If someone doesn't want to sell, you are not going to make them do so. You are simply providing a way of solving their problem, if they consider your proposed solution the best option. I'm reminded of something Jerry Puckett mentioned on Episode 21 of the BiggerPockets podcast[37] when he said (and I'm paraphrasing here), "I only want to buy someone's property if they are excited to sell it to me. I never want to steal a property."

---

[37] http://www.biggerpockets.com/show21

Smart—and ethical.

Does Wholesaling Require Money?

Yes and no.

I decided to include this chapter on wholesaling because I believe wholesaling *can* be a legitimate way to get started investing in real estate, and there are tactics for wholesaling with no money, as we will discuss. Furthermore, wholesaling can be an exceptional way of making enough cash to start buying your first rentals, flips, or commercial properties, so I do believe it fits nicely in a book about creative real estate investing.

Here's the truth about the money needed to wholesale real estate: it *is* possible to wholesale a deal or two without any money, but truly building a marketing system that consistently provides leads will probably require some cash. But that's okay, because you can start small and scale up, using your profits to reinvest into more and more marketing. So yes, you can wholesale with little to no money.

However, if you have no money and want to start wholesaling, it's going to take some additional hustle. Again, this is all about trading creativity for cash! You may need to start by driving for dollars and handwriting a lot of letters (we'll talk about these tactics soon). You may need to start by working directly for a single cash buyer and/or accepting very low margins on your first few deals. You *If you have no money and want to start wholesaling, it's going to take some additional hustle.* may need to get out there and start knocking on doors. Hustle is the name of the no money down game. However, once you land your first deal, I'd encourage you to use that money to start testing out some of the "paid" ways of attracting leads, such as direct mail.

That said, wholesaling is probably never going to be 100% free. Even if you stick with "free" methods, such as driving for dollars, empowering others to find deals for you, or using an agent to make offers on HUD properties, you will likely still incur some costs, such as gas, business cards, stamps, or earnest money. However, these costs are nothing compared with what you could earn wholesaling—and nothing you can't save up by putting in a few extra shifts at work or selling some stuff from your garage!

Let's start with perhaps the most important aspect of the entire wholesaling process: finding a great deal. If you don't have a great deal, the best-looking business cards are just garbage. If you don't have a great deal, a list of 100 cash buyers is just a list of names. If you don't have a great deal, your ambitions as a wholesaler are just dreams.

A great deal is the foundation. Let's start building it now.

Marketing for Great Deals

The "secret" to making good money from wholesaling is being able to consistently find great deals. This also happens to be the most difficult part of the wholesaling experience. The fact is this: *great deals are hard to find.* It takes work. It takes effort. It might even take a little bit of cash. However, finding great deals *is* possible, and you are about to learn how it's done.

The following are nine of the most common strategies for finding real estate deals. Keep in mind, you don't need to do all nine, or even the majority. Start with just one—whichever one your budget allows. Then as deals start coming in, reinvest your profits to go bigger!

1. **Driving for Dollars** – "Driving for dollars" is the name investors give to the practice of simply driving around an area

looking for potential good deals. The benefit of this strategy is that it costs very little to accomplish and is a true example of using creativity to replace cash when investing in real estate. However, I don't mean just driving aimlessly down random streets hoping someone comes out and asks you to buy their home. You will need to pick the right neighborhoods in which to wholesale, find properties that look prime for wholesaling (long grass, boarded-up windows, etc.), locate the property owner using public records, and get in touch with that owner. To read a great two-part, in-depth series on driving for dollars, don't miss Chris Feltus's blog posts "Driving for Dollars Bible: Finding Distressed Properties and Marketing"[38] and "Driving for Dollars Bible 2: Tracking Down Owners and More Tips."[39]

2. **Direct Mail** – Direct mail is the practice of sending mail to a targeted list of people with the assumption that a very small percentage of them will respond to the campaign. Direct mail is not cheap, but most real estate investors who consistently use direct mail marketing find it to be the most scalable form of marketing, paying back many times more than it costs. For example, you may spend $2,000 to print and mail 2,000 letters, receive 100 phone calls from motivated sellers, and actually find three properties worth wholesaling for $5,000 each. Therefore, that $2,000 could net you $15,000 in revenue. For a much more in-depth look at the world of direct mail marketing, don't miss the post "The Ultimate Guide to Using Direct Mail Advertising to Grow Your Real Estate Business"[40] on the BiggerPockets blog.

---

[38] http://www.biggerpockets.com/renewsblog/2013/05/03/driving-for-dollars-bible-part-1/

[39] http://www.biggerpockets.com/renewsblog/2013/05/10/driving-for-dollars-tracking-owners/

[40] http://www.biggerpockets.com/renewsblog/2014/04/09/direct-mail/

3. **Your Website Through SEO** – Whether trying to figure out how to keep their dog from "going potty" indoors, learning how to solve a Rubik's cube in ten minutes or less, or trying to identify what that terrible noise is coming from their car engine, people turn to the Internet in hopes of an answer. As we've noted numerous times already, wholesaling is about solving problems, so it would make sense that people would search the Internet for a cure to their home difficulties. And they do, every day. Getting your website in front of these people can produce an incredible supply of motivated leads. However, getting the search engines to offer your website to searchers is an art form in itself. This practice is commonly known as SEO (search engine optimization). Although the search engine algorithms change constantly, the key to success in SEO is to make your website easy to read and to fill it with amazing content, centered on specific topics people are searching for. Remember, the search engine's job is to provide searchers with the best solution to their problem, so make your website the best, most obvious solution to their problem, and it'll start to appear at the top of the search results.

4. **Online Marketing** – In addition to SEO, you can reach Internet searchers by paying to be at the top of the search results page (or on people's Facebook wall) by paying for ads, a practice known as pay-per-click advertising. For a few dollars per click (you typically only pay when someone clicks the ad), you can get targeted leads to your website.

5. **Signs** – Let's step away from the virtual world for a minute and talk about one of the most controversial methods of attracting leads: signs. The most common type of sign used by wholesalers is known as a "bandit sign." These are those ugly, yellow, often handwritten "I want to buy your house for

ca$h" signs you see plastered all over street signs. At BiggerPockets, we recommend *not* using these. Although they may work, they are almost always illegal to post. Additionally, they make neighborhoods look terrible. As real estate investor Marty Boardman states in his article "Bandit Signs: The Ugly Way to Advertise Your Real Estate Business"[41] (this is a *must read* article for anyone interested in using bandit signs), "As responsible real estate investors we should be cleaning up our neighborhoods, not littering them with illegal signage." I couldn't have said it better myself.

There are other signs you can consider using, legally. For example, renting a billboard with an "I buy houses" message can get the phone ringing, Similarly, placing a magnetic sign on your car can get your name and number out there.

6. **The MLS** – The MLS is where the majority of homes in the United States are listed for sale. (In reality, the MLS is not *one* thing, but rather dozens of small lists owned by real estate brokers that, when combined, we refer to as the MLS—but that's getting a little too deep for this conversation.) Chances are, if you are searching Zillow.com, Trulia.com, or Realtor.com, you are actually searching (mostly) the MLS. When a home is listed on the MLS, that generally means a real estate agent is behind the listing and will get paid a commission by the seller (which means it is usually commission-free for the buyer to purchase real estate). This also means you can use a real estate agent on the deal, and that person also gets paid by the seller—so using an agent just makes sense.

I won't say that finding wholesale deals on the MLS is

---

[41] http://www.biggerpockets.com/renewsblog/2011/10/06/bandit-signs-the-ugly-way-to-advertise-your-real-estate-business/

impossible, but because of the exposure homes on the MLS have, competition is much greater, especially in a hot market, like much of the United States is experiencing today. However, hidden gems can be found on the MLS if you look carefully enough, act quickly, and negotiate intelligently.

7. **Craigslist** – Craigslist has truly taken the world by storm. This website, which unashamedly looks like the Internet circa 1995, is currently the country's tenth largest website, with more than 60 million people using the site each month in the United States alone.[42] Craigslist is essentially the world's largest classified website, where people of all walks of life can post their needs, their wants, and what they have to offer. You can find, buy, sell, trade, or rent anything, ranging from cars to spouses, chainsaws, and houses. The best part is this: Craigslist is totally free (unless you are posting a job opening or rental in certain cities, which is where Craigslist makes its money). Every real estate investor should be using Craigslist on a daily basis. Because of the site's popularity, posting "I buy houses" ads is a no-brainer. Additionally, looking there daily for owners who list their homes as for sale by owner (FSBO) is also a no-brainer—and you can do it in just a few minutes or even automate it using a website such as www.ifttt.com.

8. **FSBO** – Many homeowners decide to sell their properties without listing on the MLS and simply stick a sign in the yard or post an ad in the newspaper. These properties are known as FSBOs, or "for sale by owner" properties. Most FSBO homes are priced too high or have no equity, but wholesaling is a numbers game, so the more houses you look at, the better chance you have of finding a great deal.

---

[42] http://www.craigslist.org/about/factsheet

9. **Empowering Others** – The final strategy I wanted to share might be the most powerful: leveraging other people's talents, time, and skills to bring deals to you. After all, your circle of influence is relatively small, but the more people you work with, the larger your collective network is, and the more potential deals you'll be able to find. There are a variety of ways you can empower other people to find deals for you, including offering a finder's fee to others, talking with your local mail carrier, working with other wholesalers, and just letting everyone meet know what you are looking for.

I hope that these nine strategies will give you a good place to start in looking for deals. However, keep in mind that this is only a sampling of what's possible. Get creative with your marketing. Talk to other real estate investors or listen to their interviews on the BiggerPockets Podcast and discover what works for them. Continually test, continually tweak, and continually grow. Consistency is key when marketing for wholesaling leads and imperative when trying to build a sizable real estate wholesaling business, so spend the vast majority of your time on marketing, and you'll have more deals than you'll know what to do with—and that's a great problem to have.

"Consistency is key when marketing for wholesaling"

Is Wholesaling a Job or Investing?

Before we get too deep into the specifics of assembling a wholesale deal, I want to talk about the elephant in the room: is wholesaling *really* investing? Does it belong in a book about creative real estate investing?

Who cares?

Wholesaling is not passive, but neither is flipping or landlording. Nearly every worthwhile aspect of real estate investing involves some level of work, and the systems you create are what define how much work that is. Some wholesalers work far fewer hours than most landlords because they've established the proper systems to handle the majority of their business. This is where I want you to be—and this is where you *can* be. I believe at its core, wholesaling *is* a job. If you stop working, it stops producing.

However, it's a job that can help you raise cash for future investing while also giving you the skills you need to become a *great* real estate investor. By mastering the art of wholesaling, you master the art of marketing for deals, which most real estate investors never excel at.

Perhaps the greatest benefit of wholesaling is that you are able to cherry-pick the best deals (those that fit your long-term plan) to hang on to, while wholesaling the rest. If you can create a marketing machine that consistently churns out great leads, you can wholesale 90% of the properties you find, keeping 10% for flipping or long-term buy and hold. Because you'd be able to get such deep discounts, this would only accelerate your wealth-building activities and lead you to financial freedom that much more quickly.

So who cares if it's a job or investing?

If you love doing it, do it. If you don't, then don't.

How Much Money Can a Wholesaler Make?

Ah, so we come to the real reason you are reading this chapter!

Of course, no one is in the wholesaling game because it's just a fun hobby. Wholesalers work their tails off, because good money can be made. But how much?

Defining a "typical" wholesale fee is hard, but most wholesalers I know try to make a minimum of $5,000 per deal—and some make a lot more. In the end, it all comes down to how good of a deal you can get. The larger the spread between the price you pay for a property and the price you sell it for, the more money you make, and the more deals you do, the more money you make.

One of the biggest mistakes most new wholesalers make is forgetting one simple fact: **a wholesaler needs to sell at wholesale prices!** Because the primary buyer for a wholesale deal is another real estate investor, a wholesaler must come to the table with a better deal than what the other investor can get on their own. For example, if a typical three-bedroom, two-bath house in Cougar Town sells for $150,000, and an investor wants to get such a house for $110,000, the wholesaler had better get it for even less than $110,000. If they can get it for $105,000 and sell it for $110,000, they could make $5,000 (less fees). If they can get if for $90,000, they could make $20,000 (less fees).

A wholesaler must come to the table with a better deal than what the other investor can get on their own.

Your success as a wholesaler starts with finding a great deal. The old adage of "you make your money when you buy" rings especially true for the wholesaler. So how do you know what a great deal is?

For this, **it all comes down to the math.**

Don't worry if math was not your strongest subject in high school. The math I'm about to teach you may seem overwhelming at first, but in reality, this is fifth grade math. You can do it. I'll show you how.

Wholesaling Math

You don't have to be a nerd to understand math, at least not wholesaling math.

The process is actually not that difficult, and I believe anyone can get a firm grasp of it with just a little bit of practice, which is exactly what you'll be doing today! The next section will show you exactly how to determine the price you should offer a seller for a property and how much you can expect to make. For this, we'll return to the original story I used at the beginning of this chapter, with Beth the wholesaler, Clarence the owner, and Jackson the cash buyer.

The After-Repair Value

Let's start with the most important and fundamental number in real estate wholesaling, the ARV, which, as we first explained in Chapter Five, is short for after-repair value. As the name would suggest, the ARV is the property's estimated monetary worth if it were in good condition and comparable to other finished homes on the market. In other words, it's the value of the house after any necessary repairs have been done!

The ARV is the foundation on which most of our calculations are based. This is true because in wholesale math, we need to start at the end and work backward, accounting for the different expenses that will come up along the way. When we are finished, we will have a specific price that we, the wholesaler, should offer.

Although ARV may be easy to understand as a concept, actually determining it for a specific piece of real estate is much more difficult—and nailing the ARV is the difference between success and failure in real estate wholesaling. So how does one figure out the

ARV?

At least for residential properties, value is determined by comparing the property to other similar properties that have recently sold. This is known as the comparable sales approach and is often just referred to as "comps." However, there are several ways you can use comps to discover a property's ARV. First, let's look at how an appraiser would value a property.

Appraisers typically look for three properties within close proximity that have a similar size, layout, bedroom/bathroom mix, age, and other such attributes. The appraiser will then add or subtract values based on what the similar properties do or don't have, compared with the property being appraised. For example, check out the following image, which compares Clarence's house (the one Beth wants to wholesale) with similar homes in the area. The yellow house on the left represents the home we'll be appraising. The green, red, and maroon homes are the similar comps we will use to determine the yellow house's ARV. (Keep in mind, this is *very* simplistic, and an actual appraiser uses many more factors than just these.)

Notice that next to each feature of the comps that differs slightly from that of our subject property, we add or subtract value based on how that difference would affect the price. The appraiser determines this value after knowing what certain items add to the cost of a home.

For example, 875 Elm Street, the green home, has an extra bedroom that the subject property does not have. Therefore, we will subtract $15,000 in value from the final sale price of the green home, because the appraiser has determined that the extra bedroom has historically been proven to add $15,000 in that area. Also, the green home has an extra 100 square feet of space, so we'll also subtract $3,000 from the final value, because the appraiser has determined that adding 100 square feet is worth about $3,000 in that area. However, that same green Elm Street house has an old roof, whereas our subject property will have a new roof, so we'll *add* $5,000, knowing that a new roof on this home would add roughly $5,000. In the end, an appraiser would likely come up with a relative value of $143,000 for the green house, if it were the exact same as the 123 Main Street house, our subject property.

The appraiser would then do this for all three properties and average the results to get a fairly close estimate of what the ARV would be for 123 Main Street. In this case, the ARV average would ultimately be $147,333.

So what does this mean for the wholesaler?

I'm not suggesting you go out and become a real estate appraiser, and I'm also not suggesting you go out and hire an appraiser for every potential wholesale deal you consider.

However, by understanding the methodology an appraiser uses to determine value, you can get a ballpark estimate in just minutes, without doing as much work. In other words, if you were to do some research and discover the basic information presented in the comps image, you could look at those three properties and calculate that the value would be less than that of the most expensive comp but more than that if the cheapest. The most expensive was $167,000, and the cheapest was $138,000. Therefore, estimating an ARV in the mid-$140s would probably be close enough for your purposes.

Another common method for wholesalers who want to estimate a property's ARV is to look at square footage, determining what the average price per square foot was for the comps and applying that average to the property they are analyzing. I recommend using this strategy only when all three of the comparable sales are *very* similar to the subject property, because as we'll see in a moment, this practice can lead to some wild numbers.

Using the example of the three comps in the image, let's try to determine the subject property's ARV using just the square footage method. First, we need to figure out the price per square foot for each of the comps.

- 875 Elm Street: $156,000 / 1,500 sq. ft. = $104/sq. ft.
- 413 Oak Street: $138,000 / 1,500 sq. ft. = $92/sq. ft
- 77 First Street: $167,000 / 2,000 sq. ft. = $83.50/sq. ft.

Then, we just need to average out these price per square foot numbers. To do this, simply add them together and divide by the number of comps (in this case, three).

$104 + $92 + $83.50 = $279.50

$279.50 / 3 = $93.17

Therefore, the average price per square foot for the comps is $93.17. We'll now multiply that number by the square footage of our subject property, which is 1,400 square feet, to get the ARV.

$93.17 x 1,400 = $130,438 ARV

Whoa, that's quite a bit different from the number we determined earlier, isn't it?

Earlier, we calculated a price of $147,333. Why did this value based on square footage come in at $17,000 less? **Because the comps were not similar enough!** There were simply too many factors in those comps to use only square footage to determine value. For example, the formula didn't take into account that one of the homes had a new roof and that another one had an extra bedroom.

As I mentioned earlier, use the square footage approach only when the comps are very similar to the subject property.

Newbie tip: When you are first starting out, use several different methods to determine a property's ARV—and try to go with the most conservative one. Being too conservative and offering too little is better than overoffering and being unable to sell the property.

Because the ARV is such an important number (really, it's *the* most important number), it's vital that you get this part right. I'd highly recommend, at least when you are first beginning, that you build a relationship with a competent real estate agent (or several) so they can offer their opinion on the ARV (we'll talk about this a bit more in a moment). The more opinions you can get, the better able you'll be to estimate an accurate ARV on a property.

Finding Comps

Finally, you may be wondering how to find this comp data concerning the sale price of these properties. Here are a few ways to do so:

1. The MLS and an Agent – The MLS is a real estate agent–owned collection of data concerning all the listed, pending, and recently sold properties in a given area. Although this information is typically not available publicly, most real estate agents can print you a list of comps in just seconds, for free. Even better, when starting out, you can work *with* an agent to help you figure out the ARV on a potential deal, even though the agent won't make any money on the transaction.

How do you get a real estate agent to volunteer their time helping you? By building a strong reciprocal relationship with that agent! Network, ask for referrals, and interview agents to find the best one in your area and then let them know who you are and what you do. Next, ask them if they would be willing to *occasionally* help you look at deals and determine an ARV in exchange for you referring all leads that you can't work with to them. Then, don't bother them very often, but maintain a professional working relationship based on mutually beneficial goals.

After all, when you are operating as a wholesaler, only a small percentage of the deals that come across your desk from your marketing (which we'll get to) will be worthy of your consideration, so you can refer all other leads to the agent. This is truly a win-win relationship that can benefit both parties greatly.

2. Online Real Estate Portals – Many of the online real estate portals, including Zillow.com, offer limited "sold" comps for *some* properties. Although this information is not as comprehensive as the MLS data, it may be more than enough for what you need. Additionally, you could use any free online real estate portal—such as Zillow.com, Trulia.com, Redfin.com, and Realtor.com—to look at all the homes currently for sale. While you shouldn't use "for sale" prices in an appraisal, this can at least give you a ballpark of what homes are going for. You would then just deduct a little to come up with an estimated ARV.

3. Public Records – Finally, whenever a property is bought or sold, the transaction is recorded in the public records for anyone to see. However, even though you can search your county's online public records to find a property's most recent sale price and sale date, you will probably not discover any information on the condition or specifics of the property.

Still, you *can* use the public records in conjunction with online real estate portals such as Zillow.com, Trulia.com, and Realtor.com, which usually keep a record of old listings for a long time. Just Google the address of a property that has recently sold, and you'll likely find the original listing, complete with photos and other relevant information.

Finally, let me end the ARV discussion with this word of encouragement: **it gets easier!** It really does. The more time you spend analyzing properties, the better and faster you'll become. This is why I recommend setting aside a few moments every day to practice. Before long, you'll have a really firm grasp on the property values in your community, and you won't need to wonder—you'll just know.

This is also why keeping your "farm area" (the area you work in) as tight as possible when you are first starting out is very important. If you are trying to wholesale over an area of 10,000 square miles, you will run into a lot of problems. However, if you focus on several similar neighborhoods and property styles, you'll gain a much quicker grasp of the ARVs.

Hopefully, by now you have a pretty firm grasp on ARV. If not, I again recommend connecting with an experienced investor or agent in your community who can walk through the numbers with you.

Let's move on and discuss how you can use ARV to determine your Maximum Allowable Offer (the most you should ever pay) and profit on a wholesale deal.

We'll start with a rule of thumb— the 70% Rule.

The 70% Rule

If you are a house flipper or have spent any great length of time on BiggerPockets.com, you probably recognize the 70% Rule and understand how it pertains to house flippers. However, the 70% Rule can also be extremely helpful for wholesalers, especially those who may be wholesaling deals to house flippers—as you might do.

Keep in mind, this is only a rule of thumb and one of several methods you will use to estimate what you should offer on a property. We'll look at another method in just a moment. The 70% Rule states that you should pay no more than 70% of a property's ARV, minus any repairs.

A wholesaler also needs to subtract their fees from that number. Therefore, the 70% Rule, as it applies to wholesalers, is as follows:

Maximum Allowable Offer = (ARV x .70) - Repairs - Your Fee

Let's do some very quick math, and I'll show you how this would work in the real world.

Wholesaler Beth was considering making an offer on 123 Main Street, the property owned by Clarence that we looked at earlier. If you'll recall, we determined the ARV for that house to be approximately $147,333, after comparing it with 875 Elm Street, 413 Oak Street, and 77 First Street.

To determine her offer price, Beth multiplies $147,333 by .70 to get $103,133. She then subtracts the cost of the necessary repairs, which she estimates at $20,000, and her desired wholesale fee of

$10,000 to arrive at a maximum offer price of $73,133.

$147,333	(ARV)
x.70	(70%)
=$103,133	
-$20,000	(Repairs)
-$10,000	(Wholesale Fee)
= $73,133 Maximum Allowable Offer	

Although these numbers are fairly easy to calculate, if you want to do them quickly online, BiggerPockets has a free 70% Rule Calculator that anyone can use. Just plug in the numbers and see your Maximum Allowable Offer. To use the calculator, visit BiggerPockets.com/calc and click on the 70% Rule Calculator.

Problems with the 70% Rule

The 70% Rule assumes that 30% of the ARV will be spent on holding costs, closing costs (on both the buyer's and seller's side, such as commissions, taxes, attorney fees, title company fees, and more), the flipper's profit, and any other charges that come up during the deal. This works well in many markets, but it has some severe limitations. For example, the 70% Rule doesn't work as well for a property whose ARV is low, such as $50,000. As mentioned earlier, the 30% deducted from the ARV includes the holding costs and closing costs, as well as the profit the investor or flipper wants to make. However, 30% of $50,000 is $15,000, so following the 70% Rule, *all* the fees, costs, and profit add up to only $15,000. If the fees and holding costs were to total $10,000, that would leave just $5,000 in profit for the house flipper—and I don't know any house flipper who will take on the risk of flipping for just $5,000. So, following the 70% Rule, a flipper or wholesaler would pay far too much for the property in this case.

A similar problem with the 70% Rule exists for more expensive properties. The 70% Rule would dictate that a home with an ARV of $700,000 that needs $50,000 worth of work should produce a Maximum Allowable Offer of $440,000. However, in most markets, finding a $700,000 property for $440,000 is simply not feasible. A person who sticks exclusively to the 70% Rule will likely never find a good enough deal to ever wholesale or flip a single property.

Furthermore, some investors may spend more or less on fees and costs because of their particular life situation or location. For example, in some states, purchasing a home may require $3,000 in closing costs, while in other states, it might be $6,000. Some investors may have a real estate license, which saves them tens of thousands of dollars in commissions, whereas other investors may need to pay commissions when they sell.

Therefore, a different model may be needed to estimate the Maximum Allowable Offer. For this, we turn to the Fixed Cost Method.

The Fixed Cost Method

Another, generally more accurate method of determining your Maximum Allowable Offer based on a property's ARV is known as the Fixed Cost Method.

The theory behind the Fixed Cost Method is that all the extra charges, such as holding costs, utilities, and closing costs, can be combined to form one number, known as the "fixed costs." To determine your Maximum Allowable Offer, you simply need to work backward from your ARV, subtracting out your fixed costs, the desired profit, the wholesale fee, and the rehab expenses to arrive at your offer. The formula looks like this:

ARV − Fixed Costs − Investor's Profit − Wholesale Fee −

Rehab Costs = Maximum Allowable Offer

Of course, to do this calculation, you must understand how to determine your fixed costs. The profit, fee, and rehab expenses are fairly easy to determine, but discovering the fixed costs will take a little explaining.

The best explanation for fixed costs can be found in Author J Scott's book *The Book on Flipping Houses*[43] (published by BiggerPockets Publishing), which states,

"Fixed costs are comprised of the various fees, commissions, and costs associated with all parts of the investment project (outside of the actual rehab costs)."

The author goes on to break out these expenses into more specific detail, adding up the total of the most typical fixed costs for his business:

- Inspection Costs - $400
- Lender Fees - $1,000
- Closing Costs - $2,000
- Mortgage Payments - $2,500
- Property Taxes - $600
- Utilities - $1,000
- Insurance - $200
- Commissions - $4,000
- Selling Closing Costs - $4,000
- Home Warranty - $500
- Termite Letter - $100
- MLS Fees - $100

---

[43] http://www.biggerpockets.com/flippingbook

These costs, all added together, give an investor the fixed costs for a property. Keep in mind, these are just the rates that J Scott outlined in his book and that he has seen applied to his business—*but they may not be the same for you.* Every market is different, so spending some time determining what *your* costs would be on the listed items is important. For example, if you plan to sell to a landlord, you won't need to worry about the sales commissions, selling closing costs, home warranty, or MLS fees, because the landlord will be holding on to the property. However, if you sell to a house flipper, you would need to include these figures, because the flipper will be selling and will need to account for these numbers.

So to determine your fixed costs, create a spreadsheet with the listed items and spend some time researching what these figures would typically be for your area. You don't have to get them all perfect, but estimate conservatively. The nice thing is, after you do this once, you won't need to do it again for the same kind of property, as long as that property is in the same area. This is why we call them "fixed costs"—because we'll use the same (fixed) number every time. For J Scott, that number was $16,400. What will yours be? Take an hour to figure it out once, and you won't need to do it again for that same property type and area.

Let's return to the ongoing story of wholesaler Beth and the 123 Main Street house, and we'll look at an example of how she used the Fixed Cost Method to determine her Maximum Allowable Offer.

Earlier we determined that the home's ARV was an estimated $147,333. We also calculated, when discussing the 70% Rule, that the rehab costs would be approximately $20,000. This time, we'll use the Fixed Cost Method to come up with the Maximum Allowable Offer:

- Beth determines that the fixed costs would total $19,000.

- The house flipper (Jackson) that Beth is planning to sell the home to likes to make $20,000 minimum on any project, so we'll use that number for the desired profit.
- Beth is aiming for a $10,000 wholesale fee.
- Beth estimates the rehab will cost approximately $20,000 and gets a local contractor to agree.

Therefore,

$147,333(ARV)
- $19,000   (Fixed Costs)
- $20,000   (Profit)
- $10,000   (Wholesale Fee)
- $20,000   (Rehab Costs)
$78,333 Maximum Allowable Offer

Beth has determined that the most she could pay for this property is $78,333 using the Fixed Cost Method. If you'll recall, we determined earlier, using the 70% Rule, that Beth could pay $73,133. These numbers are fairly close, so they should give you a pretty good indication that we're approaching a good Maximum Allowable Offer for this property.

Which Method Should You Use?

The 70% Rule is a good rule of thumb in a lot of markets, but many times it will not work because prices are much higher or much lower in different areas and it simply doesn't make sense. I recommend that you take some time to run a few hypothetical analyses to practice—especially using numbers that are realistic for *your* area. Use the 70% Rule—if you can in your area—for a quick analysis, but rely on the Fixed Cost Method to ensure you make the right offer.

At this point, you hopefully have a solid grasp on the math that goes into a wholesale deal. If not, I recommend going back and re-reading this section, or visit the BiggerPockets Forums[44] and ask for assistance from the community. However, there is one sticky point in the math equations that we have not yet covered: estimating the rehab costs. Let's talk about that now.

Estimating Rehab Costs

One of the things investors who buy from wholesalers complain about the most—with regard to buying from wholesalers—is the wholesalers' inability to accurately estimate rehab costs.

"Dude, I've got this sweet deal that only needs like $5,000 worth of work" is a lie—and every cash buyer knows it. The fact is, the better you can estimate rehab costs, the more successful you'll be. Why? Here are a few reasons:

1. By understanding how much it will cost to rehab a property, you can arrive at an accurate Maximum Allowable Offer and avoid paying too much.
2. By understanding how much the rehab will cost, you can accurately present the information to your cash buyer in an easy-to-comprehend way.

The better you can estimate rehab costs, the more successful you'll be.

Therefore, we'll spend a little bit of time on the concept of estimating rehab costs. Keep in mind, this section will not be the end-all-be-all explanation of how to accurately estimate rehab costs. For that, you'll want to get a copy of *The Book on Estimating Rehab Costs: he Investor's Guide to Defining Your Renovation Plan, Building Your Budget, and Knowing Exactly How Much It*

---

[44] http://www.biggerpockets.com/forums

All Costs[45] by J Scott, published by BiggerPockets Publishing. Every wholesaler should have a copy of this book and commit to fully understanding the concepts therein. In lieu of that book here, however, I'll present my six-step process for estimating rehab costs.

1. Understand your buyer and the neighborhood – Before you start calculating how much it will cost to rehab the property, you need to understand what the final product will look like. There are high-end remodels that take months, and there are quick flips that take just days. Understanding the level of finishing to which your buyer plans to rehab the property is imperative. Also, looking at the neighborhood around the property will give you a good indication of how far the rehab will need to go. Typically, most investors do not want to go too far above and beyond the level of other properties in the neighborhood. Therefore, if the home is in a working class neighborhood with mostly working class rentals, you don't need to spend hundreds of thousands on a rehab.

2. Tour the property in detail – Next, with a good understanding of how you want the finished product to look, walk through the property very slowly. Take a lot of photos or record a video, such as with your cell phone, so you can easily recall the condition later (trust me, you won't remember it all). Furthermore, photos will help you sell the property later to the cash buyer. If the seller is home, be sure to let them know you will be taking pictures, that they're for analysis, and that you won't be making the photos public. Don't make them feel like you are invading their privacy.

3. Write down the problems in each part of the property – While you are still on-site at the property, go room by room and write down its condition, as well as any needed repairs that you notice. For example, if you walk into the living room and see carpet

---

[45] http://www.biggerpockets.com/flippingbook

that looks and smells like dog urine, write down "replace carpet in living room." Also, write down a quick estimate of the size of the room (it doesn't need to be exact; just make your best guess). Be sure to take a look at the exterior of the home as well and pay attention to any big issues, such as the condition of the roof, siding, and any outbuildings.

4. Condense your list into one of 25 categories – Next, you'll want take your comprehensive list of repairs and classify each one into one of the following 25 categories. For example, if the living room needs carpet, the bedrooms need carpet, and the kitchen needs vinyl, group all of them together and include them under "flooring."

Exterior Components	Interior Components	General Components
1. Roof	11. Demo	22. Permits
2. Gutters/Soffit/Fascia	12. Plumbing	23. Mold
3. Siding	13. Electrical	24. Termites
4. Exterior Painting	14. HVAC	25. Miscellaneous
5. Decks/Porches	15. Framing	
6. Concrete	16. Insulation	
7. Garage	17. Sheetrock	
8. Landscaping	18. Carpentry	
9. Septic	19. Interior Painting	
10. Foundation	20. Cabinets/Countertops	
	21. Flooring	

From "The Book on Estimating Rehab Costs" by J Scott. (c)2013 BiggerPockets Publishing

5. Determine a rehab price for each category – Once you have your 25 categories spelled out, it's time for the most difficult part: estimating the rehab amount for each category. However, once everything has been broken down into these categories, calculating an accurate estimate is much easier, as opposed to looking at the entire project. Let's return to the example of the flooring estimate. We may determine we'll need approximately 1,000 square feet of carpet and another 500 square feet of vinyl.

With that information, we can call up a local flooring or big-box store and ask what they charge for the flooring we need. Speaking of big-box stores—I recommend spending a lot of time in them at the beginning. Learn how much material costs for the most common repairs, such as flooring, paint, cabinets, counters, appliances, etc. To get a *really* rough estimate on how much those items might cost in labor, double the price of the materials. Again, this provides just a rough estimate, but I find it to be fairly accurate. Additionally, you can go online and search sites such as Craigslist to see how much contractors are asking for certain jobs, such as replacing carpet or painting.

6. When in doubt, ask for help – Don't be afraid to ask for help. You can do this in a few different ways:

- Visit the BiggerPockets Forums[46] and ask people there what they are paying. This is an incredibly useful tool, because you are able to get an inside look at what your potential cash buyers are spending.
- Ask a local contractor for help. Although you may need to pay them for their time, the cost of an hour or two consulting with this professional at the house would be an investment that would help you for years to come. Many wholesalers actually include a detailed, line-by-line bid from a licensed contractor with their presentation to a cash buyer, and I highly recommend doing that. The contractor will likely offer the bid for free, because there is a good chance the cash buyer will end up using them on the job, and you will not have to do the work of estimating the project.

---

[46] http://www.biggerpockets.com/forums

- Ask a local real estate investor or another wholesaler to come with you. Getting really good at estimating rehab costs quickly is an important skill to have, so consider working on your first deal or two with someone who has been around the block and can share their knowledge.

How Accurate Do You Need to Be in Your Rehab Estimates?

As close as you can, but not perfect.

After all, prices vary wildly on rehab jobs depending on the contractor used, so you don't necessarily need to know the precise price. As most house flippers and homeowners know, one contractor may bid $20,000 on a rehab while another bids $40,000. You don't know what kind of contractor your cash buyer will use, so don't think you need to have the number exact.

On Episode 21 of the BiggerPockets podcast,[47] we talk with wholesaler Jerry Puckett about how he estimates rehab costs. In that interview, he states, "If I'm not swinging the hammer, I don't need to count the nails." In other words, do the best you can, but don't spend dozens of hours getting to some mythical perfect number.

The important thing is not to tarnish your reputation by estimating *way* too low or too high. If you tell a cash buyer that a home needs $5,000 worth of work, and after their inspection, they realize it needs a new roof, siding, foundation, paint, carpet, and cabinets, you *will* hurt your reputation and will likely never work with them again.

However, if you said that same job needed $40,000 of work, and

---

[47] http://www.biggerpockets.com/show21

the cash buyer estimates $50,000, this will not completely damage your reputation—though you may need to adjust your fee, renegotiate with the seller, or find another cash buyer who can get the work done for less.

So take the time needed to learn how to estimate the rehab costs and calculate a ballpark figure. Let the cash buyer count the nails while you move on to your next property.

It Gets Easier

Finally, one last tip about estimating rehab costs: *it gets easier.*

After several deals, you will be able to look at a property and within minutes offer a ballpark figure to your cash buyer. So don't sweat it too much at the beginning—just follow the six-step process I outlined, and you'll do just fine.

Remember, if you want to really perfect your skills and have the most success as a real estate wholesaler, be sure to pick up a copy of *The Book on Estimating Rehab Costs: The Investor's Guide to Defining Your Renovation Plan, Building Your Budget, and Knowing Exactly How Much It All Costs* [48] by J Scott and BiggerPockets Publishing.

The Difficulty of Being a Wholesaler

As you may have noticed by now, the formulas that house flippers and landlords use to determine their Maximum Allowable Offer is similar to the formulas you'd use as a wholesaler, except you have to offer less than they do, because you need to incorporate your fee into the offer to make sure you get paid. In this regard, a wholesaler's job of finding deals is much more difficult than that of a

---

[48] http://www.biggerpockets.com/flippingbook

buy-and-hold investor or a house flipper. The wholesaler must identify a great deal and then get an even better deal to cover their fee.

A wholesaler is therefore competing not only against retail buyers, but also against every other investor out there, and is at a disadvantage because they need to get the properties for even lower prices. Don't let this discourage you, though, because this may not be as tough as you think. Most landlords are not marketers. Most flippers are not marketers. Most retail buyers are not marketers. *To be a great wholesaler, therefore, comes down to your marketing skills*, which we covered earlier.

At this point, you should have a real solid understanding of the math involved in a wholesale deal and can determine roughly how much you should pay for a property. Now the time has come to turn the theoretical into the practical and learn how to negotiate with sellers.

Making Your Offer and Negotiating with Sellers

At this point, you've met with a motivated seller, looked at the property, determined its ARV, estimated the repair costs, and figured out your Maximum Allowable Offer. Now you need to present your offer to the seller.

But how?

This section will walk you step-by-step through the process of presenting and negotiating deals with motivated sellers. I'll warn you right now: at the start, you may be terrible at this step, but that's okay! Negotiation is an art form that takes a lot of practice to master, so consider every negotiation practice for the one to follow and just do your best.

Presenting Your Offer

Once you have your Maximum Allowable Offer, you must present it to the sellers. This can be done in person or over the phone (or even via email/fax/snail mail)—whichever you feel will make the seller the most comfortable. Personally, I believe an in-person offer is best, but in time, you'll find what works best for you.

I think asking the seller, "What do you believe this home should sell for in its current condition?" is a wise way to start.

Then wait.

Likely, they will respond with a high, "dream" number. Most sellers know that in a negotiation, you will talk them down, so they will probably start high. However, asking this question is key, because it will give you a point of reference. You can pose this question over the phone the first time you talk with them (which is not a bad idea), but I also recommend asking them right before you make your offer. Get them to name a price. Maybe it will be completely reasonable, and you can simply shake hands and move on, but more likely, it will be high.

At this point, a great thing to say is something along the lines of "Gee, Bob, that's quite a bit higher than I can go. Is that the best you can do?"

In almost every case, no matter what the negotiation, the person will drop their initial price and say something like, "Well, I can go to $___, but no lower."

At this point, you can begin the real negotiation. Of course, you may want to present an initial offer that is lower than your Maximum Allowable Offer, which will give you room to move up. However, if you offer too low to start, you risk insulting the seller and losing the deal altogether. This is the game of negotiation. Thousands of books have been written on the art of negotiation, so I can barely scratch the surface here. However, here are a few quick tips that have worked well for me and other investors when negotiating with sellers:

Build rapport – I don't suggest that you be disingenuous, but work to build a solid relationship quickly with the motivated seller. You don't need to come out swinging right away, but find some common ground and let your personality shine through.

Look for their pain point – Although your biggest motivator is probably price, it may not be the seller's primary motivator. Discover *why* a seller wants to sell, and find a solution that solves their problem while giving you the price you need. For example, if you are talking with a motivated seller who is overwhelmed with the management of the property, speed may be far more important than price. Look for cues that show you what their *true* motivation is, because what they say may not always be what the real issue is.

Listen more than you speak – Negotiations can be awkward, so your natural inclination will be to want to talk. Don't. Listen and ask questions. Let the other party speak as much as they can and want, because every word they say can help you get a better deal.

Blame it on the higher authority – If a motivated seller sees you as a rich shark, they will have a hard time discounting the price to a reasonable price because in their mind, "you can afford it." However, if you can shift the blame for the low offer onto someone else, you become an advocate *for the seller,* and the higher authority becomes the "bad guy." For example, let the seller know that your partner/cash buyer needs to spend X amount or they won't do the deal. This can keep you in the seller's good graces while enabling you to negotiate strongly.

Ask, "Is that unreasonable?" – This is one of my favorite negotiation strategies. No one likes to appear "unreasonable," so when you ask, "Is that unreasonable?" the person typically feels compelled to say, "No, I don't think so."

Be okay with walking away, but don't – Generally, the person who is more desperate in a negotiation is the one who loses, which is why you need to be okay with walking way. That said, just because you don't *need* to get the deal, you should not walk away too easily. Negotiate, negotiate, negotiate as long as possible to get what you want.

For a great article on negotiation, check out "How to Negotiate: 7 Real Estate Negotiation Tips"[49] or for a great podcast on negotiation, don't miss episode 77 of the BiggerPockets Podcast, "Negotiating Your Way to 1000 Wholetail Real Estate Deals with Michael Quarles.[50]"

One of two things will happen after negotiations: you will either come to an agreement or you won't. If not, don't consider it a loss, and continue to follow up with the person. Many wholesaling contracts have been won months after the initial negotiation when the seller comes to grips with the true value of their property.

If they do agree to your terms, it's time to sign the contract.

Signing the Contract

A contract is a legal document that states the terms agreed upon by both parties in the transaction. Generally, I recommend that when you are going to meet with a seller, you fill the form out in its entirety

---

[49] http://www.biggerpockets.com/renewsblog/2010/03/24/7-tips-for-better-real-estate-negotiation/

[50] http://www.biggerpockets.com/renewsblog/2014/07/03/bp-podcast-077-negotiating-way-1000-wholetail-deals-michael-quarles/

so that once you have agreed on a price, you don't need to hang around filling out paperwork—this gives the seller a chance to get cold feet. Simply leave the price line (or other negotiable terms) and the signature lines blank.

If you don't already have a real estate contract, here are a few places you can obtain one:

1. The BiggerPockets FilePlace[51] (free)
2. Title/Escrow Offices (usually free)
3. Office Supply Stores
4. Via a Lawyer
5. From Other Investors
6. Through Real Estate Clubs
7. From a Real Estate Agent (especially if offering on a bank foreclosure)

Real estate contracts are state-specific legal forms, so even though you can find these kinds of forms abundantly online for free, including and especially on the BiggerPockets FilePlace, keep in mind that **these are just general samples, so spend a few dollars to have your attorney look over the form** you plan to use to make sure it is valid and applicable for your location. While your contract can be fairly short and simple, be sure that it states at least the following:

- Address and legal description of the property
- Seller's name
- Buyer's name
- "And/or assigns" on the buyer's name line, if you'll be assigning the property (I'll talk about this later)
- Price

---

[51] http://www.biggerpockets.com/files

- Closing date
- The day's date
- Earnest money amount (I'll cover this soon)
- Contingencies (I'll also talk about this)

Earnest Money

Your earnest money is a deposit paid to the seller showing your good faith to complete the contract as promised. Although you may or may not be required by law in your state to include earnest money, you will probably want to include some just to ensure the contract is fully legal (check with an attorney to see what contract law requires in your state). The amount of earnest money you put down depends on whatever the seller feels okay with, because you want to offer as little as possible. In fact, many wholesalers put down just $1 as a technicality and leave it at that. Other wholesalers put nothing down. However, your seller may ask you for a little more, and you will have to decide if this is the right thing to do based on the situation.

No matter what the amount is, I recommend never giving the earnest money directly to the seller (though if it's an extremely small amount, such as $1, feel free). Instead, a third party—usually the title company—should hold the earnest money. This way, the seller can't just steal your money and sell the property to someone else, thereby forcing you to take legal action—which likely wouldn't be worth it. Having a third party hold the earnest money protects you.

Contingencies

A contingency is a clause within a contract that states under what circumstance you are allowed to back out of the contract legally. Although you could put pretty much any contingency in your contract (e.g., "this contract is contingent upon the seller wearing a black shirt on the day of closing"), I recommend skipping anything

198

weird and using only the minimum required to make sure you are safe. Many wholesalers use a contingency such as "This agreement is subject to finding a qualified buyer" or "This agreement is subject to approval from my partner" or "This agreement is subject to a thorough inspection of the premise and approval of its condition." (Please understand, these are just examples. Your contingencies must be legal in your state, so be sure to have your contract reviewed by an attorney.)

You should never use a contingency to tie up properties only to later back out of the agreement because you hadn't done your homework. Contingencies are meant to protect you legally in case something goes wrong; they are not to be used to compensate for your irresponsibility. This will only damage your reputation. If you've done your homework and the math correctly, you should not need to use your contingency.

Once you have your contract with the seller signed, it's time to move on and get that property into the hands of someone who can purchase it. We call these people "cash buyers," and the next section will dive into exactly what they are, how to find them, and the process for getting paid for your work in finding the great deal.

Finding and Working with Cash Buyers

At this point, you've found a great deal, negotiated with a seller, and signed a contract for a great price—now you need to get rid of that contract and get paid! This section will show you how to find real cash buyers for your next wholesale deal and explain what to do with them once you've found them.

Introduction to Cash Buyers

First of all, what do we mean by "cash buyer," and why is it important?

A cash buyer is any person or business that can buy your wholesale deal from you without needing to use traditional financing. In other words, when you present the perfect deal, they do not need to run to the bank and wait six weeks for a loan to close. In a wholesaling situation, that typically doesn't work.

However, this doesn't mean you need to find only wealthy people with millions of dollars in the bank (though that would be nice). Anyone with access to cash financing has the potential to be a great cash buyer. Specifically, that could mean any of the following:

- Someone who uses a hard money lender to fund a deal (see Chapter Five)
- Someone who uses a line of credit that they already have access to (see Chapter Four)
- Someone who has a partner who can fund the deal with cash (see Chapter Three)

So how do you find a cash buyer? We'll get to that in just a moment, but let's first talk about one of the most common questions every new wholesaler seems to ask:

Which comes first, finding cash buyers or finding the deal?

The Chicken or the Egg?

It's a classic question: which came first, the chicken or the egg?

In the wholesaling world, it's "which comes first, the cash buyer or the deal?" After all, the deal is what will attract the cash buyer, but without the cash buyer, you can't do anything with the deal. This question stops many new investors from ever taking action.

The problem is compounded because of all the wholesaling gurus out there. You sign up for a free seminar on wholesaling, get upsold to a weekend boot camp, and the only thing you get out of it is "how to build your cash buyers list."

Here's a little secret: finding cash buyers is the *easiest* part of the entire wholesaling process.

Seriously, you are about to be amazed at just how easy (and cheap) it is to find more cash buyers than you'll ever be able to sell to. I believe this is why the gurus use the phrase "cash buyers" so frequently; they know that if they can convince you that finding cash buyers is the solution to all your problems, you'll pay big money to find out that "secret," and you'll be convinced that you are a legit wholesaler—and that they are a god (they're not!)

Every day, newbie wholesalers straight from the latest and greatest guru boot camp jump onto the BiggerPockets Real Estate Marketplace[52] and place an ad saying, "I'm looking to build my cash buyers list!" However, after that initial post, we never hear from them again. They were duped into thinking that if they only had the cash buyers, everything else would fall into place. It's very sad.

The truth is, cash buyers are everywhere, but cash buyers do not mean anything if you don't know how to get a good deal.

So, we're back to the original question: which comes first, the cash buyer or the deal?

It doesn't matter. You can find the deal first and easily find a cash buyer for it later *or* you can easily find the cash buyer first and then go find the deal.

---

[52] http://www.biggerpockets.com/marketplace

Either way, finding the deal is the hard part, and you need to understand that. Once you realize that locating cash buyers as a first step or last step doesn't change your outcome, the issue becomes much less important. So, do both. Find cash buyers while you are marketing for good deals.

The one major benefit to finding cash buyers first is being able to gain some free education from them on what makes a good deal. Therefore, if you really need an answer to the question "which comes first?" **go find *one* cash buyer who is willing to train you on what they want from a deal.** Then go out and find a perfect deal for them. You can build your business from there.

How Many Cash Buyers Do You Need?

For whatever reason, the phrase "cash buyers list" gets tossed around a lot in the guru circles. It sounds sexy, doesn't it? "There are hundreds of investors on my list, fighting for all my good deals."

This is just stupid.

You don't need hundreds of cash buyers. You probably don't need dozens. A great wholesaler only needs a small handful, because their deals are good enough. They don't need to shop their deal around to hundreds of potential cash buyers, hoping one of them is stupid enough to pay a ridiculous price for a worthless property. If you have a good enough deal, you won't have a problem marketing that deal.

A great wholesaler needs only a small handful of cash buyers, because their deals are good enough.

I *do* recommend having a small handful of cash buyers because every investor has their own niche and strategy, as well as location. Cash buyer Bob may be looking for single-family homes in Seattle that he can buy for $150,000 to

$175,000 that he can flip, while cash buyer Belinda may be looking for single-family homes in Tacoma that she can buy for $80,000 to $120,000 that she can rent out. Therefore, what is good is having cash buyers in multiple niches and strategies to cover all your bases and handle whatever legit deal comes across your plate.

However, again, you don't need hundreds (though as long as you are not using the search for cash buyers as an excuse to think you are doing real work, you should always be updating your cash buyers list).

When you are chatting with potential cash buyers, it's smart to "prequalify" them. Many people who claim to be cash buyers may just be newbies, fresh out of a guru boot camp and posing as someone who can make things happen. When wholesaling, you only want to deal with legitimate cash buyers who are experienced and trustworthy. I recommend interviewing all potential cash buyers and asking questions such as

- How many deals have you purchased in the past six months?
- How quickly can you close?
- Are you working with other wholesalers?
- What kind of properties (specifically) are you looking for?
- What kind of LTV are you looking for?
- What kind of property condition will you accept?

These questions will help you identify who is a legitimate cash buyer and who is just a wannabe tire kicker.

Let's get into the actual practice of finding cash buyers. As I said, I think you'll be surprised at just how easy this can be. In fact, let me give you ten different ways.

Ten Strategies for Finding Cash Buyers

1. **Landlords on Craigslist** – Head to your local Craigslist "houses/apt for rent" section, and you'll instantly find a huge list of property owners, along with their phone numbers and property addresses! True, not all these owners will be cash buyers, but most investors with enough knowledge to buy multiple properties could probably also pull off a cash deal.

2. **Real Estate Clubs** – At your local real estate investing club or landlord organization, you'll likely encounter a variety of cash buyers. Simply strike up conversations with everyone you can and ask what their specialty is while letting them know what you do. Chances are you'll find some great business relationships this way!

3. **Real Estate Agents** – Real estate agents have some special tools at their fingertips that nonagents do not have, especially with respect to searching recent sales. If you can build a solid relationship with an agent, they can easily supply you with a list of all recent cash sales in any nearby location. Although they may not be able to get you the property owners' names (though perhaps they can), they *can* easily give you the property address, and you can simply search the online public records for names and personal addresses.

4. **Online Lead Capture** – If you have a website, you can easily set up a "lead capture form" that allows potential cash buyers to submit their name and contact information if they'd like to be added to your buyers list. You can drive traffic to your webpage through social media, online or traditional advertising, your BiggerPockets Profile, or good ole Craigslist.

5. **Public Record** – Perhaps the most comprehensive source of cash buyers, your local public record's office has information about every sale in your area. Although every county is different in the way this information can be accessed, you can begin by doing a Google search of your local county assessor's page or

records office. When a house is purchased with financing (in a state that uses mortgages), two primary documents are recorded with the county: the deed (which shows the change in ownership) and the lien from the loan. On a cash sale, there will be no lien from the loan. Another good way to search the public record is through a local title company. They can provide you (with or without a fee) a list of properties that have sold without a mortgage lien.

6. **Craigslist Ads** – Unlike a lot of real estate gurus, I don't recommend creating fake real estate listings just to get the phone ringing. However, creating ads on Craigslist for future wholesale deals is more than appropriate and should get people calling. A simple subject line that states "Wholesale real estate deals at 70% ARV" and a short ad explaining that you wholesale deals with that criteria should get people's interest and connect you with some serious cash buyers.

7. **Courthouse Steps** – When a person buys on the courthouse steps, they must have all cash. Therefore, anyone bidding on a property at the courthouse is a cash buyer. Get to these auctions early and strike up some conversations, hand out business cards, and create some long-lasting business relationships.

8. **Hard Money Lenders** – Hard money lenders can be a terrific source of referrals to cash buyers because if you'll recall, a cash buyer doesn't necessarily need to have all the cash in the bank and could use hard money to close with all cash. Connecting you with their clients is in a hard money lender's best interest, because you, in turn, will provide them with additional business. It's a win-win-win.

9. **ListSource** – While Listsource.com is the most common place for wholesalers to create a list of potential motivated sellers, it can also be a great place to find cash buyers. Use the site to search for properties purchased within a specific period of time and focus on absentee owners who didn't record a deed of trust. This will give you a list of cash buyers for just pennies per item.

(Special thanks to Michael Quarles from YellowLetters.com for that tip!)

10. **BiggerPockets** – Finally, our very own BiggerPockets.com is an incredible place to find and screen potential cash buyers. Among our more than 200,000 members are thousands of cash buyers looking for deals on our site every day. Visit and use BiggerPockets.com/meet to find members in your area and start building relationships with those who appear to be big players in the real estate space. You can also use this space as a great opportunity to build your reputation by engaging with other members, answering questions, and getting involved.

Should You Present Your Deal to One Cash Buyer or Multiple?

At this point, you should have a solid list of potential cash buyers for your deals. But how do you present your latest deal to them—approach them all at once or one at a time? Should you send out a large blast email to everyone on your list or pick up the phone and call each one individually?

Likely, you'll discover a strategy that works for you, and there is no one "right" way to do this. However, let me offer a few tips.

- An email is not as personal as a phone call, so I recommend using the phone when first starting. Once you have an established track record with your cash buyers, you can start sending them emails or text messages. Also, find out which form of communication your various cash buyers prefer and cater to them as much as possible.

- If you send out your potential deal to everyone, you may get some interest, but you may also annoy those who would not be interested in that kind of deal. So consider pitching the deal only to those who seem most serious.

- If you have a great relationship with one of your cash buyers, consider offering the deal to them first, thereby providing them a limited moment of exclusivity. This might help deepen your relationship and show them you value their business.

How to Present the Deal to the Cash Buyer

Hopefully you've used your smart marketing and negotiation skills to snag a killer good deal so you don't need to pitch the property in desperation. However, you do need to adequately present the information to your cash buyer so they can make the best decision possible, which means you need to prepare. This is especially true when pitching a deal to a cash buyer for the first time, because you have not yet built up the trust needed for them to simply "take your word for it."

I recommend that when you are presenting to a cash buyer, you present your deal in the form of an easy-to-understand packet of information the cash buyer can look through. The more work you do in advance means the less work they have to do, which means chances are greater that they will say yes. At a minimum, I'd recommend including the following in such a packet:

- The property address and details
- Financial outlook (for either flip or rental)
- The property condition and repairs needed
- A bid from a contractor for the cost of repairs needed (optional, but very helpful!)
- Photos of the property, inside and out
- Comparable sales for the neighborhood to justify your assumed ARV

Although assembling this information may seem like a lot of work, it's actually much easier than you might think if you use the

BiggerPockets Real Estate Investment Calculators found at BiggerPockets.com/calc. If you are selling to a flipper, simply enter the basic information into the Fix and Flip Analysis & Reporting Tool and print out the brandable PDF that will outline the financial projections for the property. If you are selling to a landlord, run the numbers through the Rental Property Calculator to show the cash buyer the property's long-term potential.

Remember, the less work you make your cash buyer do, the better chance you have of selling the deal to them and making the profit you desire!

Cash buyers will want to check out the property for themselves, so you will need to arrange a time for the buyer to do a walk-through. If they like what they see and agree to the terms you have offered, you have a deal and can move on. You may need to negotiate with the cash buyer, so be prepared for the discussion and know exactly how low you can go and still make an acceptable profit.

Getting a Nonrefundable Fee from Your Cash Buyer

You've found the deal, negotiated a great price, found a cash buyer, and your cash buyer has agreed to work with you because of your fabulous marketing package. Now what?

Next, it's important that you receive a nonrefundable fee from your cash buyer to transfer the contract to them. Why? Because you don't want them to back out of the deal! You likely put down some earnest money on the deal yourself, so requiring this fee of your cash buyer is necessary to make sure you don't lose your money if they get cold feet.

The amount you ask for depends on the size of the deal, your relationship with the buyer, and your negotiation skills. I recommend asking for at least $1,000 and potentially up to $5,000, if not more.

After all, your cash buyer has seen the property and inspected it to their satisfaction before handing over the deposit, and they are paying in cash, so they should have no major reason to back out. If they balk at the fee, consider finding a new cash buyer or lowering the amount, but make sure they understand that the only reason you require such a fee is to protect yourself from something going wrong at closing.

Finally, you'll sign the necessary paperwork and begin the process of closing. This can get a little complicated, so hang with me as we discuss the different legal ways you can wholesale a property to a cash buyer.

Legally Putting Together a Wholesale Deal

A wholesale deal can be legally put together in many different ways—and the method you use will depend on the transaction, your state laws, and other circumstances. For this reason, I want to give you a thorough overview of the different ways of closing a wholesale deal so you can choose the one that works best for you and your location.

The different strategies for putting together a wholesale deal can be a little confusing, so I want to return to the story I provided earlier in the chapter about wholesaler Beth and the deal she bought from Clarence and sold to Jackson. In that example, Beth used an *assignment*, so I'll talk about this method first.

Assignments

To "assign" a contract simply means "to give" the contract to someone else, which Beth can do because of the way she wrote up the contract.

Recall that Beth told Clarence that "either she or a business associate of hers will buy the home,"which she communicated on the official purchase and sale contract by writing, "Beth and/or assigns" in the blank space meant for the buyer's name. In other words, the legal "buyer" of the property will be Beth and/or someone to whom she assigns the contract. Contract assignments are done every day in the business world, and there is nothing illegal or immoral about them—as long as you aren't trying to deceive someone and pull the wool over their eyes.

Note that Beth clearly lets Clarence know that she may not be the one who actually buys the house. As for Clarence, he doesn't care. He's just happy to get out of the double payment he has been paying and move on with his life. To avoid complications later on and stay 100% ethical, you must let your buyer know if you plan on wholesaling the deal (though using terms such as "wholesaling" might just confuse them, so stick with "I or a business partner of mine will buy it" to keep things simple).

Many wholesalers do not use assignments when closing a wholesale deal, primarily for two reasons:

1. Most bank REOS (foreclosed properties being sold by a bank) do not allow "and/or assigns" to be written in the contract, so the assignment strategy is not an option.
2. When doing an assignment, the seller will likely see on their closing paperwork the assignment fee that the wholesaler will receive. Depending on the size of the fee, the wholesaler may prefer to keep that fee amount private as to not "rock the boat" with the seller.

In addition to assignments, two other strategies are commonly used by wholesalers: *simultaneous closing* and *back-to-back closing*. **This is where things get a little confusing.** You see, different real estate investors have different names for these strategies. No doubt, someone will read this and say, "That's not a simultaneous closing" or "That's not a back-to-back closing" or "that's not a double closing!"

The fact is, **there is no standard definition for either of these strategies.**

Go ahead and search online, and you'll see what I mean. But since I'm the one writing this book, I figure I should establish some set terms and definitions and try to synchronize the concepts for this industry. Keep in mind, however, that in the end, what you call a strategy doesn't matter. The concepts are what you need to know, so keep reading!

Both techniques involve *actually buying the property yourself*, walking (physically or just hypothetically) to another room at the title company (or attorney's office), and *immediately selling the property* to a buyer, often within just minutes (though it could be several days).

The difference between the two techniques (simultaneous and back-to-back) lies in the way the deal is funded. You see, purchasing real estate requires money, and even if you only own a property for ten minutes, you still need to pay for that property. So how do you come up with the funds?

The answer to that question is what differentiates these two techniques. Let's examine each one individually so you can better understand the difference.

Simultaneous (Double) Closings

A simultaneous closing—also known as a double closing—uses the end buyer's cash to fund *both* purchases. In other words, the end buyer's cash will fund your purchase, and then that same cash will pay you for the property.

Confused yet? Let me try to explain by adapting the Beth, Clarence, and Jackson story from earlier in the chapter.

Clarence shows up at the title company to sign the documents to sell his home to Beth. In the next room, Jackson is waiting to buy the property. Jackson's bank sends a wire transfer of $95,500 to the title company, and he signs the paperwork to buy the property from Beth. Beth then receives (on paper) $95,500. She then goes back to Clarence in the adjacent room and buys the property from him for $85,000. In other words, Beth simply sold the property at almost the same time as she bought it, used funds from the end buyer.

Do you see a problem here?

Simultaneous closings are fairly uncommon today because they involve someone selling a property before they even own it, and Beth does in our example. Yes, the title company can figure out the paperwork side of things (hopefully), but most are uncomfortable with this kind of arrangement. Furthermore, some states do not legally allow this kind of funding. Therefore, most wholesalers skip the simultaneous closing and instead rely on either an assignment or a back-to-back closing, which we'll explore next.

Back-to-Back Closings

A back-to-back closing is very similar to a simultaneous closing, but rather than using the buyer's funds for the purchase, the wholesaler uses other funds to make the deal happen.

Most people I know, however, don't have hundreds of thousands of dollars just sitting around, waiting to be used for a few hours to fund a quick wholesale deal. So if a wholesaler doesn't have such funds readily available, how can they come up with the cash needed for a back-to-back closing? Of course, the wholesaler only needs the funds for a few hours. Luckily, there is a simple solution:

transactional lenders.

A transactional lender is a special kind of lender who funds back-to-back closings. They wire money to the title company for a short time (a few days max) and the title company uses that money to buy the property and then resell it a few minutes later. These lenders can be found nationwide, but I recommend starting with a local hard money lender who has experience with these kinds of transactions. (Be sure to check out the BiggerPockets Hard Money Lenders Directory[53] for the Internet's most comprehensive list of such lenders.)

Because the transaction is almost risk free for the lender, finding transactional lending should not be too difficult. The fees for these transactions typically range from 1% to 3% of the total transaction, so be sure to figure those extra costs into your wholesaling math.

One negative aspect of the back-to-back closing involves the extra costs that must be incorporated into the deal. Because the wholesaler is actually legally purchasing the property (if only for a few minutes), charges can add up quickly in addition to the transactional lender's fee. These costs include additional document preparation fees, additional title company/attorney fees, and additional recording fees, among others. These can easily add an extra $1,000 or more to your bottom line, so be sure to factor these costs into the deal. You don't want to wholesale a property for $3,000 only to pay $2,000 to a transactional lender and another $1,000 in extra closing costs!

Whichever method you use to close the transaction, understand that you will really only need to figure this stuff out once. It may feel cumbersome and confusing in the beginning, but I encourage you to push through, and you'll find all the answers you'll ever need just

---

[53] http://www.biggerpockets.com/hardmoneylenders

by *doing*. And if you truly get stuck, visit the BiggerPockets Forums[54] and ask for help from others. There are plenty of wholesalers who would love to help you reach your goals, so don't be afraid to ask.

Getting Paid

Finally, the title company or attorney who closed the deal will issue a check for you, probably on the day of closing (though it may take a day or two). I'd encourage you to use this check to continue growing your real estate wholesaling business, reinvesting your profits into more marketing and potentially more help to manage the increased business. Remember, a single deal is not going to get you any closer to financial freedom. You need to develop a business that can consistently provide leads and generate a great income. So resist the temptation to buy that new car, and reinvest the profits into your future instead.

Wholesaling Conclusion

In this chapter, we've walked through the entire wholesaling process from beginning to end. We've examined the details of a wholesale deal, from the basics of finding incredible deals to smart marketing tactics. We looked at two different methods of analyzing a potential wholesale deal. We covered negotiation and making an offer, as well as signing the contract with the seller. Finally, we talked about finding cash buyers to sell the deals to, as well as the legal techniques you can use to make that transaction a smooth one.

At this point, I hope you have all the knowledge you need to begin wholesaling your first or next deal. Wholesaling requires dedication, hard work, smart marketing, and a commitment to success to build serious income from the business. If you feel up for

---

[54] http://www.biggerpockets.com/forums

the challenge and want to add wholesaling to your toolbox, you now have everything you need to make it happen.

Throughout this book, we've looked at almost a dozen different strategies for investing in real estate with little to no money of your own. Although wholesaling may not easily fit within the strict definition of "investing," I included it because it *does* fit the business of a real estate investor—and it can be done with little to nothing out of pocket. I want to make sure that when leads come in for your business, you have every opportunity to succeed with them, so I hope this chapter on wholesaling can help you earn more income in your business and live the life of your dreams.

In the next and final chapter of this book, we'll tie all these different strategies together and help you think creatively about the entire world of financing. I believe Chapter Ten will be the most important chapter of this book, so continue when you are ready!

CHAPTER TEN: CREATIVE COMBINATIONS

The final strategy I want to talk about isn't actually a strategy at all but a mindset, and I firmly believe this is the most important chapter in this book.

It's important to understand that the approaches covered in these chapters are not the only cut-and-dried ways of investing in real estate creatively but represent just a sample of what's possible when you mix and match different methods.

In Chapter One, we talked about how creative real estate investing is similar to a handyman doing a construction job. The handyman could face a lot of different problems at a job site, so his having a fully stocked toolbox is essential. This is the theory behind this book and why I've spent the previous nine chapters exploring the various "tools" you can use in your creative real estate investing business. After all, the more tools you have at your disposal, the larger projects you can tackle and the more successful you can be.

However, as every handyman knows, seldom is one tool enough to finish a job. Instead, a combination of tools and creative thinking is needed to truly make

The more tools you have at your disposal, the larger projects you can tackle.

something beautiful. This chapter is, in my opinion, designed to help you see the big picture and change the way you think. Creative real estate investing is not about using one tool or another, it's about using whatever tool you need to make something amazing.

Therefore, the final strategy is one I like to call "creative combinations," because it involves mixing and matching the various approaches discussed in this book to fit the deal or property before you.

Explaining exactly what a creative combination is is difficult, because there are millions of possibilities. Instead, let's look at a few brief examples of how aspects from different strategies could be combined to help you close more deals with less (or no) money out of pocket.

Example 1: Partner/Hard Money to Refinance

Jillian found an incredible deal on a fourplex that she can get for just $80,000, but she has very little cash to work with. Additionally, the fourplex is vacant and has some cosmetic issues that will need to be fixed before any units can be rented out. Jillian estimates these repairs will cost approximately $20,000, but she has done her research and feels this fourplex will provide almost $2,400 per month in income, so she knows the cash flow will be amazing, and she'll have a good amount of equity to deal with.

To make the deal happen, Jillian reaches out to several local hard money lenders. However, she finds that even though the deal is incredible, because it is her very first deal, lenders are too nervous to cover the full purchase price *and* the repairs. Instead, they offer to fund just the purchase price if she can come up with the repair money.

Jillian doesn't have anywhere close to the $20,000 she would need for this, but rather than saying, "I can't afford it," turning her brain off, and giving up on the deal, she starts to think creatively and asks herself, "How can I afford it?"

So Jillian comes up with an idea. She draws up a solid business plan on paper for renting the property, showing the potential for the property and including bids from contractors, and takes the plan to a family friend, Grant, who has expressed some interest in real estate. When she explains the deal to him, Grant is impressed and convinced, so he and Jillian form a partnership to get the property together. Their partnership looks like this:

1. The hard money lender will fund the purchase price of the property for a one-year term.

2. Grant will fund the entire $20,000 repair budget and holding costs until the property is rented, but he will be purely a "passive investor" in how the deal is run and the property is managed. Grant will also use his credit and income to help secure long-term financing.

3. Jillian will manage the rehab, deal with the bills and contractor, and "manage the property manager" for the life of the partnership.

They end up closing on the property, and after all is said and done, they have roughly $110,000 total into the property, including taxes and fees, though not a penny came from Jillian. Because of

Grant's strong income and credit, the two have no problem obtaining a refinance for 75% of the appraised value (it appraises for $150,000) after six months, so their new loan ends up being for $112,000. Now, not only does Jillian have no money invested, but Grant also has all his money back, so they can go out and repeat the process.

The property brings in $2,400 per month in income, and after all expenses, there is over $600 per month in positive cash flow—all on a no money down deal for Jillian because she used a combination of creative financing methods. Remember, this is just an example of what's possible. Do you see any other ways Jillian could have accomplished this deal? This is your chance to start thinking creatively!

Example 2: The Master Lease Option to Partial Seller Financing

Roland is interested in a 12-unit apartment complex that has been listed for several months. The owners seem motivated and have dropped their price several times, starting at $650,000 and lowering it down to $550,000. Roland has only a few thousand dollars to work with—clearly not enough for the 25% down payment his local bank would require.

So Roland decides to investigate further. He speaks with the property owners and discovers that they live nearly 2,000 miles away, where they moved after a job relocation. They love the income from the property, but because of the distance and trouble they are having with their resident manager, they decided to just get rid of the property.

Each of the 12 units rents for $1,000 per month, but the property is currently only half full and has been this way for quite some time, though Roland knows that this is primarily because of the lack of good property management.

Roland knows this is a great deal, so he presents an offer to the sellers, and they accept. The deal looks like this:

1. Roland offers to do an MLO on the property for the first three years, with an option to buy at $500,000.

2. Roland and the couple agree to a monthly amount of $3,000 for the master rent payment.

3. During the first year, Roland works hard to turn the property around. He manages the property locally, gets rid of the bad resident manager, increases occupancy, and even raises the average rent to $1,200 per month, per unit. The total gross income ends up at $14,400. By the end of year one, after spending 50% in expenses, he is left with $7,200 to pay the $3,000 monthly rent to the owners, leaving him with $4,200 every month in cash flow.

4. Roland saves half of the $4,200 in cash flow for years two and three, saving up over $50,000 just by managing effectively. At the end of year three, he approaches his local bank with a plan to purchase the property. The sellers agree to carry a 15% second mortgage for $75,000, he puts up the $50,000 he has saved, and the bank gives a 75% LTV mortgage for $375,000. Perhaps best of all, the appraisal comes back at a value of just over $1,000,000.

In this example, Roland successfully purchased a 12-unit apartment complex, built over $500,000 in equity in three years, and created a substantial amount of cash flow income that comes in each and every month, using nothing but his creative thinking and managing skills.

Example 3: 203k to Cash Out Refinance to

Partnership Flip

Adam has never purchased any real estate before in his life. He works a busy day job as a law clerk in Denver but has made plans to leave the job and become a full-time real estate investor as soon as possible.

Adam finds a home that is in severe need of updating located about ten minutes from where he lives. It has two bedrooms and a "bonus" room, all painted bright green, with some outdated carpet, bad lighting, and other cosmetic issues. The home is listed at $145,000, but he is able to get it under contract for just $125,000 because of how long it has been on the market. Adam obtains a 203k FHA rehab loan, which allows him to include the $35,000 of repairs into the cost of the loan for just 3.5% down ($5,600) on the total loan amount. Because a 203k loan is only applicable for owner occupants, Adam and his family decide they will move into the property and make it their first home.

He navigates through the red tape, and after several months, he has a fully remodeled home located in a great neighborhood that now has three bedrooms (he added a closet and a door to the "bonus" room to make it a legal bedroom).

Because he is paying the mortgage *and* the expensive MIP, Adam decides to refinance the home after one year into a conventional loan. Thanks to the work he has done and the addition of the third bedroom, the home now appraises for $245,000, so Adam takes out an 80% LTV loan, obtaining a new mortgage for $196,000, paying off the 203k completely, and taking out an extra $38,000 from the cash-out refinance. Ironically, because Adam is no longer paying private mortgage insurance, his monthly payment increases by only $24, despite the higher loan amount.

Adam then takes his $38,000 and uses part of it to invest in a flip with a partner, using a hard money loan to fund the purchase price, while Adam and his partner each put in $30,000 to fund the repairs. With this foray into flipping, Adam is able to leave his day job and jump full-time into real estate, and he did it all for just $5,600, the down payment on the original 203k loan.

Wrapping Up: Where to Go Next?

As you can see from these examples, buying real estate with little to no money down is possible, but it's not always easy. It takes creativity and a combination of tactics and strategies to make a successful no (or little) money down deal come together.

If at any point while reading this book you've felt confused or overwhelmed, that's okay! These are not always easy concepts to fully understand, and there is a reason not everyone does creative real estate investing. There's nothing wrong with investing in real estate the slow, conservative method—in fact, I encourage it!

However, for many people, waiting five, ten, or 20 years to start investing is simply not an option. As I mentioned at the beginning of this book, real estate offers you the ability to trade cash for creativity like no other wealth building opportunity, so don't be afraid of trying out new creative strategies.

In your creative real estate journey, you will run into walls, doors, and dead ends. You will encounter problems, questions, and irritations. You'll face uphill battles, downhill coasting, and desert wandering. It's all part of the creative real estate investor's life. However, the way you respond to problems is what will define your future. Will you give up, shut down, and go back to what you are comfortable with? Or will you seek answers and press on?

Real estate is not black and white; it's a colorful tapestry made up of the experiences of millions of investors.

The great thing about BiggerPockets, and the reason we believe it's more important than any real estate book, is that it's constantly changing and fully interactive. Real estate is not black and white; it's a colorful tapestry made up of the experiences of millions of investors. BiggerPockets is the online embodiment of that tapestry and the central hub of the conversations that can turn a newbie into a seasoned pro.

Each of the techniques found in this book, along with many more, can be found in everyday conversations with investors who live and breathe this stuff. Every one of these techniques is discussed every day on BiggerPockets by experienced investors who love to help others gain better insight into the industry and find greater degrees of success. We firmly believe that community is the best teacher, and BiggerPockets is the ultimate platform for that community to exist.

Want to know more about using 203k loans, lease options, seller financing, or any of the other topics we covered in this book? Visit the BiggerPockets Forums[55] and start asking about them! The rules change daily, and new strategies are always emerging. No book, even this one, could ever hope to compare to real-life conversation. So go to BiggerPockets.com and search the site for past discussions or start new threads and be a part of the conversation. The information is there, just waiting for you to log on and change your life.

Final Thoughts

I'm so honored that you've stuck around all the way to the end, and I hope that you now have a solid understanding of at least nine different methods an investor could use to invest in real estate without a lot of cash. I hope also that you finish this book with a larger toolbox than when you started and that you can use

---

[55] http://www.biggerpockets.com/forums

that toolbox to build your future.

Remember, the larger your toolbox, the more tools you can fit inside, and the greater your chance of being able to build something incredible with your future.

You have the tools. You have the toolbox.

Now go and build something amazing.

MORE FROM BIGGERPOCKETS

If you enjoyed this book, we hope you'll take a moment to check out some of the other great material offered by BiggerPockets, including the free eBook *The Ultimate Beginner's Guide to Real Estate Investing*, co-written by Brandon Turner, author of The Book on Investing in Real Estate with No (And Low) Money Down. BiggerPockets is the web's premier destination for real estate investing education, networking, and deal making. With more than 150,000 members, hundreds of thousands of forum discussions, and hundreds of free downloadable files, BiggerPockets is home to everything you need to succeed in real estate!

Sign up today—it's free! www.BiggerPockets.com

FREE: The Ultimate Beginner's Guide to Real Estate Investing

The Ultimate Beginner's Guide to Real Estate Investing is a free guide designed to help you build a solid foundation for your venture into real estate. Over the eight chapters of this book, you'll learn how to best gain an education (for free), how to pick a real estate niche, and how to find, fund, and manage your newest real estate investment. Get it free today at **BiggerPockets.com/freeguide.**

The Book on Flipping Houses

The Book on Flipping Houses, written by active real estate fix-and-flipper J Scott, contains **more than 300 pages** of detailed, **step-by-step training** perfect for both the complete newbie and the seasoned pro looking to **build a killer house flipping business**. Whatever your skill level, *The Book on Flipping Houses* will teach you **everything you need to know** to build a profitable, efficient house flipping business and **start living the life of your dreams. Get it** at BiggerPockets.com/flipbook.

The Book on Estimating Rehab Costs

One of the most difficult tasks for a real estate investor is the process of estimating repairs. To help you overcome this obstacle, J Scott and BiggerPockets pull back the curtain on the rehab process and show you not only the cost ranges and details associated with each and every aspect of a rehab, but also the framework and methodology for estimating rehab costs. You'll discover how to **accurately estimate all the costs** you are likely to face while rehabbing a  home as well as what upgrade options you have to provide **the biggest bang for your buck**. Whether you are an experienced home renovation specialist or still learning how to screw in a light bulb, this valuable resource will be **your guide to staying on budget, managing contractor pricing, and ensuring a timely profit. Get it at BiggerPockets.com/rehabbook.**